EATING FOR COGNITIVE POWER

SUPER FOODS, RECIPES, SNACKS AND TIPS TO
BOOST YOUR BRAIN HEALTH, FOCUS AND
MEMORY

John Torrance, Productivity Coach

Your Free Gift

This book includes a free bonus booklet. All information on how you can quickly secure your free gift can be found at the end of this book. It may only be available for a limited time.

TABLE OF CONTENTS

INTRODUCTION

You know that annoying friend who just seems to get everything done? You know who I mean, because the minute you read that first sentence, a face popped into your head. Yes, I'm talking about the person who seems laser sharp *all the time* and who never skips a beat. As much as that person drives you nuts, deep down inside you'd like to be just a teensy bit more like that, wouldn't you? Okay, admit it. Maybe a whole lot more like that. A little more success wouldn't do you any harm, or your wallet, either! Am I right? (I'm paid to know these things.)

Well, your old grandma was right all along: *You are what you eat.* Mounting research is proving her true. After years of too many drive-through orders on jam-packed days, too many snacks consumed while binge watching your favorite TV episodes, and too many salads skipped in favor of mac n cheese, you're definitely feeling the effects. What is more, you're a walking showcase of what you're eating. The muffin top and love handles bear ample testimony of your lifestyle. Personally, I'm not interested in the shape of your body. I'm more interested in the shape of your brain--your body just tips you off about having become an accident looking for a place to happen.

You feel bloated much of the time. Your work is suffering. Your relationships are suffering as well. You just don't feel like going dancing or engaging in that game of touch football. You skip breakfast most days and opt for a pastry you scarf down during your commute.

What lunch? Mid-mornings and mid-afternoons you crash and need a *Snickers* to keep your productivity humming. You are tired in the morning and tired in the evening, but when you go to bed, your brain isn't switching over to the *off* position. This is no way to live. Literally. Your brain is a ticking time bomb, and one day it will result in a cerebral incident (stroke) or, just as bad, permanent fog (dementia). Those kinds of life-changing incidents are actually years in the making and offer no quick fix. The fix is now. Today. Tomorrow.

Let's face it. You need to engage. Your relationships need you to be all in. Your kids beg for attention and if they don't get it, they act out in unacceptable ways. Your work requires more and more time, more and more effort. You need to be increasingly productive to stay competitive. Whatever the demands you're juggling, you need to be at your absolute best, and I can relate.

Not so long ago I was in your shoes. Every one of those symptoms described my daily life, and I knew I had to do something to pull myself up by the bootstraps and make a change. I simply couldn't juggle all the balls in my life, and, all too often, the one I dropped caused serious consequences. It took some research. I did a lot of experimenting. What I learned knocked my socks off. Every symptom I described related directly to what I was eating...or not eating! In this world of way too much information, I had not been getting the information I needed. There is a connection between food and the brain, and when I discovered that connection, my world shifted.

All of a sudden, something I'd known all my life got spun around in just a little different perspective, and it changed the way I thought, the way I acted. For me it was seeing a colleague my age succumb to a stroke, his life permanently changed in the blink of an eye. The once vital friend I enjoyed on adventures was confined to a wheelchair and communication became a whole lot more difficult. His mind didn't seize the words he wanted to say. His filter was gone, and what came out of his mouth alienated many of his friends. He became lonely and bitter.

And I vowed to change. Just like that. I began to change. Not in a day. Not drastically. I started reading my way to better health. I started experimenting with what I read. I started changing the way I ordered food on a menu at my favorite restaurant. I started making grocery lists based on what was good for me, rather than impulsively picking things off the shelf that looked good on the spur of the moment. Slowly but surely, I changed. You can as well.

What you eat must supply the raw energy your brain needs for optimal function. That does *not* include a diet of cheeseburgers and soft drinks. Eating the right foods increases the cognitive power of your brain, the thinking power. It reduces the risk of Alzheimer's disease, one of the newest plagues of our generation. It removes brain fog leaving you in a slump at your desk. It improves your memory. The *right* food = less brain fog, more brain function. The *right* food = less dementia, more focus. Food = brain function (or lack thereof)..

When I made just a few changes in the way I looked at food and its intake, an elemental shift took place. I ate better. I performed better. I

3

slept better. I decided I needed to make this information available to others. I began with friends and family. When they raved over what I discovered, I tried to branch out, but my circle of influence was not wide enough. How should I change that? I first looked at the wonderful world wide web.

Here's what I discovered: Too many gurus want to charge you megabucks for an online course. There's a whole lot of talk, and who has time for that? It's certainly not what *I* had in mind. I wanted to put together an easy to follow, life-changing program, for just the cost of a book, making it enjoyable to read, and easy to follow. Here's my plan for you: Read the information so you understand why you've been feeling low. Study my findings on superfoods, and how easy it is to incorporate them into your life. Try my recipes. Then turn around and teach this information to your family. Chart your progress. You will be amazed.

The **benefits** of this program are hard to beat. You will find easy to digest information and enjoy reading it! You will feel better. You will probably look better...you're not opposed to dropping a few pounds, are you? You will earn kudos from clients and your boss, who will be impressed with your soaring productivity.

Here's my promise to you: I *will not* make claims I cannot prove. I *will not* bore you with too much background information...though I will provide a lot of detailed research in a glossary at the back of the book. I will coach you to better health. That's a keyword. Did you catch it? *Coach?*

4

- A coach inspires, never drives.

- A coach causes you to want to change, not forces you to change.

- A coach stays right there with you when the going gets tough.

I want to be all these things for you. Coaching is my life. I want to take all those skills I use every day to help CEOs and top executives improve their careers, then mix it with the research I've discovered, and roll it up into an easy program for you to follow. I want to walk with you to a state of better health with increased productivity. Are you with me?

It all begins with you, my friend. You were drawn to this book for a reason, and it just takes turning the page to Chapter One and then diving in. Start reading, and then eating a new way to improve your brain. Think better. Think smarter. Act better. Act smarter. See where I'm going with this? You'll find in the next few pages everything I've promised and more. What's *the more*, you ask? It's my tips and tricks, starred information to help you get every last drop of benefit from this book. It's the in-depth information you'd hear, and never absorb, in a fancy high falutin online course. And those little nuggets are where you'll find the gold.

So I'm asking again. Are you with me? It all starts with page one. Let's start learning about superfoods and super powers. Let's do this!

CHAPTER ONE

HOW FOOD AFFECTS YOUR BRAIN

If you're normal, you've probably been eating with an eye on your waistline, not with a focus on your brain. But what has your waistline done for you lately? Your brain, on the other hand, works tirelessly to control each breath and each beat of your heart, perception of each sight in your field of vision, each sound around you. It's called the **Autonomic Nervous System.** It's where a lot of your body's work takes place, and while you're not supervising each transaction directly, your brain requires high-performance nutrients to do this well. This is Coach John telling you: *To be a brainiac you need to eat brain food.* It's true. There are certain foods good for your brain, and certain foods your brain would rather you avoid. You're going to be learning some new concepts, and that's good. I don't expect you to know it all ahead of time. I had to research this for myself, and my goal is to feed you these bits of knowledge in easily digestible portions.

★ Each time you see a term in **bold,** you'll know it's a term covered in your glossary. My promise is to make this engaging and readable, with lots of information you can read if it triggers a desire to learn more. That means some of the heavy lifting is in the back of the book. I suggest you read it once, go through

7

the glossary, and then read it again, pencil and paper in hand, ready to really begin this adventure of discovering better health.

★ Eating for brain health may sound radical, but research studies have proven that the foods you eat are an important part of not just your health, but your brain function and the prevention of cognitive problems. Certain superfoods are now known to improve cognitive function--which includes boosting your memory, improving your decision-making abilities, decreasing response time, and get this, even boosting your mood. These foods are the basis of clean eating. It's a way of eating that may not only save you hours in the kitchen, but give you more hours of a meaningful life, so pay attention. Read the next sentence two or three times, it's just that important:

What you eat has a far-reaching impact on your brain.

- The food you eat is the source of brain energy. What you eat affects how much energy your brain has to work with, in both its autonomic function and its cognitive or thinking function.

- The food you eat is the source of the transmission of nerve impulses. Your brain needs to send messages, and it needs a chemical to pass the message along from one nerve to the next nerve to ensure it happens.

- The food you eat is the basis of sustained mental health. As of 2018, researchers have connected the dots of serotonin and gut health, and the role it plays in Alzheimer's progression. They predict that dementia will affect more than 65 million people worldwide by 2030. It is the plague of our generation and you, in your choice of what to eat, can make a difference.

Let's cover a little of the new research hitting the medical journals. I can save you some time and energy by narrowing down the plethora of information into the best articles. I'm providing a detailed list of them; you can dive in for some more intensive study if you've got the time. For our purposes, though, let me do the heavy lifting for you.

Serotonin: Nothing But the Facts

First of all, let's look at **serotonin**. Your body produces serotonin, which is a neurotransmitter regulating sleep, appetite, pain receptors and moods. Of course, the building blocks for its manufacture must be present for your body to do its job. Did you know 95% of the serotonin your body produces is made in your gastrointestinal tract (GI)? I didn't. Your bowels are lined with millions of nerve cells called neurons. Every moment of every day, a war is waged in this small arena, a war with far-reaching implications. Good bacteria protect the intestinal lining, and form a barrier against bad bacteria who march to battle, leaving toxins and inflammation in their wake. Your diet needs to give your body a fighting chance at producing serotonin by harboring good bacteria.

Remember I said it helps regulate sleep, appetite, pain, and moods? These are the very basic building blocks of a happy, well life. I experienced a time in my life when I routinely awakened each night at 2:30 am. After a while, I was running myself ragged. Upon examination, my doctor correctly diagnosed an imbalance in my system and recognized that the serotonin keeping me asleep was getting taken up too soon by a hyperactive spool in my brain. I was prescribed very low doses of a medication blocking its uptake, and voila! I started sleeping through the night again.

Too often we run the gamut of self-help through melatonin or valerian root and then jump straight to sleeping pills. This sets us on a course of either dependence on medications to put us to sleep, or a teeter-totter of sleep and no sleep, depending on when we're taking sleeping pills and when we're off them. That's not the answer. Eating foods that help in serotonin production, getting diagnosed if your brain is in a state of imbalance and replenishing your serotonin, is a much healthier reaction to the problem.

Read the extended information on serotonin in the glossary and look at regulating your levels in a healthy way.

Probiotics? Say, What?

We refer to a diet fostering good bacteria as being rich in **probiotics**. If you're like I was, it sounded like a lot of New Age mumbo jumbo, a fad that would quickly pass away. I couldn't have been more wrong! Probiotics are live organisms you consume, either by purchasing an expensive supplement or by tweaking your intake to include yogurt or other fermented foods. Most commonly you're looking for Lactobacillus and Bifidobacterium. These good bacteria limit inflammation, improve the absorption of nutrients and activate neural pathways traveling constantly between your gut and your brain. I'll bet you didn't see that one coming. Neither did I. The relationship between

10

my stomach and my brain required some research on my part. Let me give you the *Reader's Digest* version.

Startling discoveries linking a healthy gut to dementia offer even more incentive to change your diet. Some gut bacteria actually accentuate the buildup of brain proteins, significant since amyloid and tau proteins comprise the plaque in Alzheimer's disease. Research on mice suggests that simply changing your diet may reduce these amyloid plaques and decrease inflammation. What do you suppose happens next? Exactly. Your memory improves. I don't know about you, but I found that pretty compelling evidence for needing to mend my ways.

Some diets affect the presence of these probiotics. The Mediterranean or the Japanese diets, both stand in stark contrast to the typical Western diet of processed foods, unhealthy amounts of salt, way too much sugar, and lots of red meat. The **Mediterranean Diet** stems, naturally, from countries like Greece and Italy along the Mediterranean Sea. It is recommended by both the World Health Organization and the Mayo Clinic. It is characterized by a lifestyle of more vegetables and fruits, whole grains, beans, nuts and seeds, and olive oil, as opposed to other processed oils. Many of these unprocessed foods are fermented, packed with natural probiotics.

The **Japanese Diet** includes more fish, vegetables, and fruit. It involves eating mindfully and slowly. Japanese recipes emphasize simple seasonings as opposed to heavy sauces. Food is served in smaller dishes. Well, that makes portion control a whole lot easier, doesn't it? The secret to satiation lies in utilizing more variety. A staple food is

11

combined with a soup, a main dish, and a few sides. The staples are rice or noodles. The soup is typically a miso soup with seaweed, shellfish or tofu and vegetables in a fermented soybean stock. The main dish would be comprised of fish, seafood, or tofu with small amounts of meat, poultry, and eggs. Sides consist of vegetables, seaweed, and raw or pickled fruit. I couldn't see myself eating like this and I, for sure, couldn't see my wife cooking all this.

See what's missing here? Both of these diets eschew the same staples of the Western diet: red meat, lots of dairy, processed foods, lots of salt and sugar. Both diets require a fundamental shifting of the taste buds, and while they may seem like radical departures from your regular household menus, you don't have to jump into this with both feet. The good news is that some very basic tweaks in your current diet will do the trick. We'll get into more of that later.

Antioxidants

When I first heard this word, the analytical side of my brain took it apart. Anti meaning against. Oxidants. Was that oxygen? Why would I want to do anything against oxygen? Silly me. The word was *oxidant,* like oxidizing metal into rust. I was a little slow on the uptake here. Of course, I'm all against rusting out my brain. Millions upon millions of chemical reactions are taking place in your body every single day. In the process, some compounds become unstable, with a free, or extra electron. (Think back to your ancient class on organic chemistry with the descriptions of protons and electrons in each element.) That tiny free electron is known as a *free radical.*

12

Oxidants containing free radicals are the leftover sludge when your body metabolizes and interacts with a rich stew of building blocks, creating all new chemicals from the food you eat. The antioxidants balance the oxidants in your bloodstream. Let me break this down: Your body is a complex machine with all kinds of checks and balances, moves and counter moves. The antioxidants are warrior compounds your body ingests, like ascorbic acid (vitamin C), or synthesizes to keep that nasty oxidation in check. One body-synthesized **antioxidant** is glutathione, made from three amino acids: glutamine, glycine, and cysteine.

Not only does your body produce oxidants in everyday living, you are also exposed to more in smoking, radiation, and other pollutants. You acquire even more as a result of stress and alcohol consumption. When the balance of antioxidants and free radicals gets out of whack, **oxidative stress** results. The stress weakens cell membranes. It damages connective tissue and collagen (think your knees!). It is a precursor to cancer and cardiovascular disease. It is a culprit in autoimmune diseases like arthritis and psoriasis. It affects diabetes. It doesn't take a genius to realize this is bad.

This is why we make the effort to include foods rich in antioxidants into your diet. These antioxidants are loaded with essential fatty acids that stimulate and strengthen brain cells. Some people flock to health food stores and buy supplements.

★ Here's a clue, though. You don't need them. Eat a diet rich in antioxidants, and save that money.

What exactly is on your healthy menu? I'm glad you asked. Read on to Chapter Two. As your coach, it's my job to feed you small bites of information, lure you into appropriate action, and slowly win you over. Unfortunately, you aren't meeting me face to face, and I'm not speaking with you directly. This book is your lifeline. It's a lot cheaper than individual counseling sessions, and you can digest the information at the convenience of your schedule. The danger is one you know all too well.

How many times have you tried to change before? How many other self-help books mock your efforts and line your bookshelves? To be successful this time around requires a meeting of our minds. I'm writing to you, gentle reader, so read this out loud if it makes it easier to imagine my presence. Think of me as your new best friend, someone who sits on your right shoulder as time moves forward, but who speaks with you as we work our way through this process of change to a healthier you.

Chapter Summary

The food you eat affects your brain.

- Serotonin is a neurotransmitter required for optimal brain functioning.

- Probiotics are essential for gut health, and that's good news when it comes to producing serotonin.

- Antioxidants, rich in essential fatty acids, combat the free radicals of oxidation.

In the next chapter, you will learn what foods to feed your brain for optimal function.

CHAPTER TWO

EATING FOR BETTER COGNITIVE POWER

The key to eating for optimal brain health isn't a hog-wild change into a whole new way of eating. It's changing things, a little here, a little there. As you incorporate these small changes into your life, you will see the benefit, and feel encouraged to another step toward better eating, better cognitive functioning. Remember. Baby steps.

In order to defend against a variety of age-related conditions impairing your memory and the general function of your brain. a good first step is to concentrate on incorporating just three nutrients into your diet. They may be new to you, and you will be wondering just what strange things you have to eat. Seaweed? Stinky tofu? Relax, my friend. I didn't go there either.

Let's begin by looking at omega-3 fatty acids, antioxidants, and **flavonoids**. We touched on some of this very briefly in the last chapter, but it's time to dive a little deeper and get serious. This is your coach saying, try it. Take a chance. Give it a week and see what a difference it makes. You'll never look back.

Omega-3 Fatty Acids

As you age, your brain experiences some normal degeneration. The old maxim of being over the hill need not apply, however, if you pay attention here. Yes, your nerve cells shrink, and nutrient-rich blood supplies in the brain are diminished over time. Inflammation complicates the situation. In response, your brain produces fewer neurotransmitters and the result is poor or patchy communication between the cells. Your memory suffers. It is just that simple. Don't be afraid, because there is a solution for that.

What if I told you that a diet rich in **omega-3 fatty acids** would make a difference? A 2014 study, published in Neurology, submitted evidence that postmenopausal women who have higher levels of omega-3 fatty acids (EPA and DHA) in their blood had increased brain volumes. Remember, smaller brain volume is linked to Alzheimer's disease. They documented a difference of one to two years of healthy functioning which their counterparts lacked. Think about what you might look forward to with an extra two years of just being there, your brain running on all four cylinders. I don't know about you, but I want to be mentally aware and able to enjoy the birth of grandchildren, and perhaps see them grow up as well. Let's get down to facts.

When scientists talk about these as being essential fatty acids, they mean that while your body can synthesize much of what it needs, it cannot make these. They must be ingested. Fish are one of the best sources, but one caveat is the danger of mercury and other heavy metal contaminants in swordfish and bluefish. Perhaps you're not fond of

16

fish? That's okay. There are other non-fish foods rich in this brain protector. Foods rich in omega-3 fatty acids include:

★ Oily cold-water fish: anchovies, tuna, bluefish, herring, sardines, mackerel, salmon, halibut, and, lake trout.

★ Leafy greens: Brussel sprouts, spinach, arugula, mint, kale, and watercress.

★ Oils: flaxseed oil, chia seed oil, cod liver oil, and krill oil.

★ Eggs.

★ Walnuts.

Antioxidants

As touched on in the last chapter, antioxidants protect your brain against free radicals. If the balance between oxidants and antioxidants in your body gets out of whack, a condition known as **oxidative stress** can result, with ensuing damage to your brain.

This becomes more important as you age. When you were young your brain shrugged off the rogue compounds known as free radicals like brushing away ants from your blanket at a picnic. Time changes things. With age, it's not so easy. Your body produces thousands of these unstable oxygen molecules every day. Add in pollutants and ultraviolet radiation, and your brain finds it more and more difficult to protect itself from the constant barrage.

If ignored, free radicals harm the body. It's a process called oxidative stress, and it leads to mental decline and a series of debilitating illnesses. The good news is your body can defend against oxidative stress by ingesting antioxidants. These substances shield the brain and its nerve cells from destruction. The goal is to keep a large supply in stock. Eat foods rich in antioxidants:

★ Vitamin C--We all *think* we know how to ingest Vitamin C. But do we? Here are some things you may not have known:

★ Strawberries are an unexpected source. One serving of strawberries can give you 20 mg, one half of your daily requirement.

★ Citrus fruits (no brainers). One orange gives you 70 mg, meeting your daily requirement. A glass of orange juice can offer up to 90 mg.

★ Chili peppers. A half-cup of chopped peppers offers almost 110 mg of Vitamin C.

★ Red bell peppers. One cup is 200 mg of Vitamin C.

★ Papayas. One serving meets all your required Vitamin C for the day.

★ Kiwis. Surprisingly, a kiwi contains more Vitamin C than an orange.

★ Brussel sprouts. Another surprise. One cooked serving is worth 50 mg of Vitamin C.

★ Beta-carotene--Traditionally we think of carrots, but three foods that weight for weight will beat them are sweet potatoes, grape leaves, and microgreens.

★ Selenium--This is a tricky one. The amount of selenium you get from your food depends on the soil in which it was grown. Brazil nuts, almonds, seeds and fish are the three top sources.

Another source of antioxidants is in **flavonoids**, and they deserve a heading all of their own. A great many fruits, vegetables, and herbs contain flavonoids that serve to reduce inflammation, reduce the risk of heart disease, and decrease symptoms of eczema. As it turns out, flavonoids are also good for the aging brain.

Researchers in 2012 at Brigham and Women's Hospital found that older women who ate large amounts of berries, experienced significantly less memory decline when contrasted with another control group. The difference, the researchers believed, was because berries are rich in flavonoids. Continuing research broadened that claim. The Foundational Medicine Review published a 2018 paper stating that flavonoids interfere with key enzymes triggering cell death. Most importantly, they protect the brain against neurotoxins and suppress inflammation of the brain.

The research is replete with raves over the role of flavonoids. The most recent research suggests they improve many cognitive skills, including memory, learning and decision making. It's also suggested these foods may prevent age-related mental decline. In the UK, 2% of the population aged 65-69 have dementia. This figure rises to one in

19

five, or 20%, for those aged 85-89. Most centenarian studies report dementia in the very old at 45 to 65%. Flip these statistics, and you realize that dementia is not natural or inevitable. 80% of people in their eighties and nearly half of all centenarians enjoy life dementia-free.

The significance hit me squarely between the eyes. I didn't have to end my life in the years of mental fog we call debilitating dementia. The choice was mine. I could enjoy a healthy diet, or reap the consequences later. I've chosen to improve my diet. My advice to you is simply this: let's do this together. When you hit the grocery store and start making dinner tonight, realize I'm doing the same thing. If it's Monday, it's fish. We'll cook alongside each other, and you'll feel the weight of my support.

Me? I'm eating all the foods rich in flavonoids that I can. These foods include:

★ Green tea.

★ Leafy greens--spinach, kale, and watercress.

★ Berries--blueberries, strawberries, and blackberries.

★ Cocoa.

★ Coffee.

★ Dark chocolate.

★ Red wine.

Vitamin E is another antioxidant worthy of its own section. It's a well-known fighter of free radicals, preventing cell damage. I grew up well aware of this lifesaver. My mother had a heart attack in early adulthood and turned to Dr. Shute, who focused on natural healing. He pioneered much of the research on this antioxidant back in the 1950s. Her prescribed regimen included large amounts of Vitamin E, and within months, her cardiologist found no trace of the previous damage. His groundbreaking research led me to appreciate the wonders of Vitamin E.

Dr. Shute lists twelve benefits of Vitamin E:

- It reduces the oxygen requirement of tissues.

- It melts fresh clots and prevents embolism.

- It improves collateral circulation.

- It's a vasodilator.

- It is known to lyse scar tissue.

- It prevents scar contraction as wounds heal.

- It increases low platelet counts.

- It decreases the insulin requirement in about ¼ of diabetics.

- It is one of the regulators of fat and protein metabolism.

- It stimulates muscle power.

- It preserves capillary walls.

- It prevents hemolysis of red blood cells.

I often wondered if his groundbreaking work has ever been verified. Current researchers are honing in on how it plays a part in brain health. A 2014 study published in the American Heart Association's journal discussed one type of Vitamin E, tocotrienol. This is found in palm oil, and it appears to have a beneficial effect in decreasing both Alzheimer's, and Parkinson's disease. It also seems to reduce the likelihood of strokes.

Vitamin E is actually a conglomerate of eight different compounds, four tocopherols, and four tocotrienols. The daily recommended dose is 15 mg or 22.5 IU and researchers prefer you get it from food as opposed to supplements. The benefits of **supplementation** are a source of contention among researchers, and initial studies of its efficacy have been disappointing.

Dr. Axe concurs and notes that Vitamin E deficiencies affect the young and the old more severely. He recommends eating two or three foods rich in Vitamin E each day:

★ Sunflower seeds: 1 cup contains 33.41 mg.

★ Almonds: 1 cup is 32.98 mg.

★ Hazelnuts: 1 cup is 20.29 mg.

★ Wheat germ: 1 cup, plain and uncooked is 18 mg.

★ Mango: 1 whole raw piece of fruit is 3.02 mg.

★ Avocado: 1 whole raw is 2.68 mg.

★ Butternut squash: 1 cup cooked and cubed is 2.64 mg.

★ Broccoli: 1 cup cooked is 2.4 mg.

★ Spinach: ½ cp cooked or 2 cups uncooked is 1.9 mg.

★ Kiwi: 1 medium piece of fruit is 1.1 mg

★ Tomato: 1 raw sliced tomato is 0.7 mg.

Other researchers added to the list:

★ Nuts and seeds: almonds, pecans, peanut butter, peanuts, hazelnuts, pine nuts, sunflower seeds.

★ Oils: wheat germ oil, sunflower oil, safflower oil, corn oil, and soybean oil

★ Leafy greens: spinach, dandelion greens, swiss chard, and turnip greens.

Let's take just a moment and talk about clean eating. It's a term that may be new to you, but it's a hot topic at our house. It means you eat your food fresh and raw as much as possible. You can find a whole website dedicated to the concept. They describe it as eating the way nature intended. Dr. Bowden is even more explicit. "It stands for eating real food made without a lot of unnecessary processed ingredients and additives. Eating foods as close to their natural state as possible. Eating foods that you could hunt, fish, gather or pluck. Eating foods your great-grandmother would have recognized. Eating food that spoils. Eating food that doesn't have a bunch of unpronounceable ingredients, whether it's labeled 'natural' or otherwise."

Don't start hyperventilating. Remember, we're taking baby steps here. Begin by choosing one favorite food on the above lists, and eat it naturally. Visit the Clean Eating online magazine. Try out one of the recipes I've included to help you along your way. Your trip to optimal health is a journey, not a destination. Don't beat yourself up, but please do let me coach you to more productivity. If I can make these changes one little step at a time, so can you. What's on your grocery list this week?

Chapter Summary

We've been taking a deep dive into the three tops things you can include in your diet for brain health and higher levels of productivity.

- Omega-3 fatty acids are your friends. They are heart-healthy fats.

- Antioxidants are found in foods rich in Vitamins C and E.

- Eat a colorful diet.

- Dip your toe into the world of clean eating.

In the next chapter, you will learn how to incorporate these healthy foods in a painless way. Still with me? Good for you!

CHAPTER THREE

BRAIN FOODS NEUROSCIENTISTS WANT YOU TO EAT DAILY

Dr. Lisa Mosconi, Ph.D., says, "To function best, the brain requires around 45 nutrients that are as distinct as the molecules, cells, and tissues they shape. The brain, being radically efficient, makes many of these nutrients itself, and only 'accepts' whatever else it needs from our diets. Put simply: Everything in the brain that isn't made by the brain itself is 'imported' from the food we eat." She advocates eating your way to better brain health. She is not alone.

Mounting evidence suggests that simple math can change your future. It's all about adding more of the good and subtracting more of the bad. Let's start with the good. We've looked at the whole subject as eating from the viewpoint of what *types* of nutrients we need to be eating, but we haven't really gone through each of these essential foods, and how to incorporate them into your diet.

★ As you read this chapter, get out a pad of paper and a pencil. Begin jotting down next week's grocery list, and let's add a few new items and put a few clean eating items into practice, shall we?

25

Fatty Fish

You already know by now that not all fat is bad fat. Coldwater fatty fish like Alaskan salmon, mackerel, bluefish, or anchovies, are all high in those omega-3 oils your brain needs each and every day. Adult women need about 1.1 grams of omega-3s daily, according to the National Institute of Health. That means that a 3-oz salmon filet will meet your daily requirement, offering about 1.24 of the two most important fatty acids, DHA and EPA. To offer a little context, your brain is about 60% fat. Studies show that DHA may help boost memory and cognition skills and that it possesses anti-inflammatory properties which are just as valuable. But what if you don't like fish?

It's time to readjust those taste buds. Rub the salmon in a mix of spices and make a lovely sauce. It won't be the healthiest salmon you've ever eaten, but it will start recontouring your taste buds for better eating. Most of the recipes are in the back of the book, but I'm including one with each of the super-foods here, just to get you used to the idea of working them into your diet.

Even my non-fish lovers like this, adapted from Real Simple:

No Way, But Well, Okay Salmon

- Turn on and preheat your oven at 500°.

- Line a baking pan with foil and drizzle it with extra virgin olive oil.

- Lay the salmon fillets in the pan and turn them to coat them with the oil.

- For the rub, combine 1 tsp chili powder, ½ tsp cumin, ½ tsp smoked paprika, 1 tbsp honey. Add salt and pepper. Rub this all over the salmon, and then place the pan of salmon in the oven.

Roast the salmon until it's opaque on the outside and just translucent on the inside, about 5 minutes. If you want it well-done, roast it for an additional 3 to 5 minutes.

While it's in the oven, prepare your sauce, which will serve as a double for salad dressing for your spinach salad. Chop two small handfuls of flat-leaf parsley or chives or mint. Place them in a small bowl, and add enough extra virgin olive oil so it pools around the herbs. Grate a clove of garlic into the bowl. Add a few splashes of red or white wine vinegar, salt, and freshly ground pepper. Stir and sample. If it's sour, add salt. If it's salty, try adding another splash of vinegar.

Plate the salmon and drizzle on your sauce.

I've included other recipes in the back of the book, but try this one and see what you think. Remember; be flexible. You can take any recipe and adapt it for your own use. Be creative.

Dark Leafy Greens

If you're not already incorporating brain greens like spinach, kale and Swiss chard into your diet, it's time to start. They're full of vitamins, minerals, fiber, and disease-fighting nutrients. Your brain will thank you. An easy way to adapt is to make fresh salads, increasing the ratio of spinach or kale to leafy red lettuce each day. Gradually you'll get used to the change and adapt.

If you're making the salmon above, try a fresh salad of spinach leaves, red leaf lettuce, walnuts, craisins, green onions, and mung bean sprouts. Drizzle on the dressing you used for the salmon, and you have a quick side that complements your meal.

If you are wrinkling up your nose and just *don't* want to eat fresh greens, try cooking the kale or spinach. Trust me, you'll like it. This isn't an especially healthy recipe, but it's a good first step for people who detest everything green.

Wilted Greens

Clean a handful of dark leafy greens. I use a salad spinner for rinsing and then draining water from the leaves.

Fry up a slice of bacon, and remove it from the pan. (I know. I didn't promise this was the best recipe...just one to train you to eat your greens.) Break away the fat so you have a few little morsels of bacon remaining.

Toss your clean spinach into the pan and saute it, adding salt and pepper. Add the bacon bits and even the pickiest eater will chow down happily.

Extra Virgin Olive Oil and Flaxseed Oil

Of all the cooking oils you can stock in your cabinet, and there are a lot, try a new one. If you watch Rachael Ray, you are familiar with EVOO. You may not be so conversant with flaxseed oil. Get some and try using it. Both of these oils are loaded with anti-aging nutrients, rich in omega-3's and vitamin E.

28

You already know I'm a proponent of eating your way to good health, so let's add this oil without using a supplement. If you are bringing home your first bottle of flaxseed oil, this is what you need to know. You may see it labeled as linseed oil, and it's okay under either label. It is extracted from dried and pressed flax seeds. If the bottle says it is virgin, it means it was done by mechanical means only, without the use of any chemical solvents. It lasts a long time, so I recommend springing for the organic or virgin brand and just pay a little more for the better processing.

It has a crisp, almost nutty flavor when used directly on your food. It is volatile and has a very low smoke point (225°), which means it isn't easy to use on the stovetop searing meat or vegetables. Rather, drizzle it over roasted veggies and eat it directly rather than cooked.

Cacao

Do you need an excuse to eat chocolate all the time? Here's your reason to rejoice! You heard me right. Dark chocolate definitely has a place in your brain diet. Look for varieties with 80% or higher cacao content, indicating it is rich in theobromine, a powerful antioxidant. The award-winning Kim Smith, director of the Brain Healthy Cooking Program, asks, "How much chocolate a day will keep dementia at bay?" Her answer may surprise you.

Here's her lowdown on chocolate:

- The darker, the better. Look for brands advertising 60-70% cacao.

- 1.0 to 1.6 oz per day is recommended. Beware of that candy bar, typically 3.5 oz in size. Split it into thirds.

- Keep a calorie count. A full candy bar each day can add 600 calories to your diet, and extra weight is *not* brain-healthy. You may end up eating less of other brain-healthy foods.

- Some like it hot. It's okay to enjoy a mug or two a day.

One eight-day limited study focused on the consumption of 70% cacao, with the added controls of receiving no antioxidants 48 hours before the study began, as well as during the study. Results did indicate an anti-inflammatory response signaled by increased cytokines. Another study involved EEG measurements after ingestion of 48 grams of 70% cacao dark chocolate and reported increased brain hyperplasticity. Take that as a good thing.

One thing they all agreed on: eat more dark chocolate.

Complex Carbohydrates

Despite the unstoppable rise of the keto diet, many nutritional experts still love complex carbohydrates. At first, I was pleased because I never met a potato I didn't love. Unfortunately, that doesn't include potatoes. Complex carbs are foods like legumes, which include beans and lentils, sweet potatoes and whole grains.

These foods feed your brain with a steady supply of glucose for a longer period of time, as opposed to peaking quickly and then fading away. Note, when I say beans, I'm not referring to green beans as much as navy, pinto, kidney or garbanzo beans. I add them to salads and soups,

30

but a favorite in our household is chili. This is a version of our favorite white chicken chili:

Smoked Chicken Chili Warm Up

1. Do yourself a favor and get a smoked rotisserie chicken when it's on sale at your supermarket. Debone it and cut it into chunks.

2. Chop and saute one onion

3. Add small cans of green chilis and diced jalapenos. (Remember you can't take out the heat once you've put it in, but you can always add more.) Let them simmer a bit with the onion.

4. Add 4 cans of rinsed white beans and 2 cans of chicken broth. (I know. Rinsing the beans removes the B vitamins, but it also removes the gas, and I'm all for that.)

5. Let it simmer for a while, and just before serving, add a can of evaporated milk.

In the recipe section in the back I'll add other recipes with legumes, but for now, just get used to the idea of eating more of them.

Berries

A great source of both fiber and glucose, berries also have a very low glycemic index, which means they help regulate glucose levels in your blood. I pick them up whenever they're on sale, and freeze what we don't eat immediately. Eat them for dessert and toss them in salads.

Blueberries are often referred to as the brain berry and are exceptionally high in antioxidants. This fruit, native to North America,

31

offers brain benefits whether you eat them fresh, frozen, canned, or as an extract.

1. Blueberries lower the risk of acquiring dementia. One recent study found that seniors who drank 30 ml of concentrated berry juice (the equivalent of 230 grams of berries) exhibited a significant increase in brain activity, blood flow, and memory compared to the placebo group.

2. They reduce the effects of Alzheimer's disease once it is diagnosed. The University of Cincinnati conducted tests in which participants ingested either a placebo powder or a *freeze-dried blueberry powder* (equivalent to one cup of berries) once a day. The adults eating the blueberry powder demonstrated improved scores in cognition and word retrieval with increased brain activity

Any way you ingest them, it is almost universally accepted that berries, and specifically, blueberries, improve memory, brain cognition, and brain health.

Water

★ If you remember nothing else you read here, commit this to memory: Water consumption is incredibly important for brain health.

Avocado

The monounsaturated fats in avocados help improve blood flow, which then contributes to a happy and healthy brain. The problem is they aren't that cheap and they turn in the blink of an eye. The key to enjoying avocados lies not in using them in the nanosecond when they are ripe and still good, but in buying the best produce in the first place.

These are my top tips in choosing the best fruit:

1. Pay attention to color. The darker the color, the sooner you must use it. Get a green one if you're not using it for several days, or a black one if you're making guacamole today.

2. Give it a gentle squeeze. A firm one isn't ready. A soft, mushy one is probably riddled with black spots. You want one that yields just a bit to gentle pressure with no soft spots.

3. Check the skin. It should not have any indentations, symptomatic of bruising.

4. Examine its stem. Peel back the little end cap and look at the color underneath. If it's green, it's ready for you to use, if it's brown it's probably over-ripe.

Now that you know how to find the best fruit, bring on the guacamole!

Pumpkin Seeds

Roasted pumpkin seeds are a favorite in our household after Halloween. We scrape and save those seeds, washing away most of the remaining strands of pumpkin. Let them dry. Drizzle them with extra virgin olive oil and a shake or two of salt. Roast them at 350° until they are slightly browned. Yum!

33

Nuts

Be a squirrel and graze on nuts throughout the day, but dieters are smart to be concerned. A handful of nuts can be up to 10% of the suggested caloric intake for a man, much less a woman. Nuts are worth the risk if you eat them the healthy way: as a garnish on salads or side dishes. Eat nuts instead of other snacks, not in addition to them. The following table will help you scale this valuable addition of brain food to healthy portions.

1 oz Nuts	Calories	Fat grams	Protein grams
Almond	168	15	6.2
Brazil nuts	184	18.6	4
Cashews	161	13	4.3
Hazelnuts	184	17.5	4.2
Macadamia	201	21.4	2.2
Pecans	200	20.1	2.6
Pistachios	160	13	6
Walnuts	184	18.3	4.3

Did you notice the one ounce serving size? That's not settling onto the couch with a large package of cashews, eating half the bag and feeling smug about how good they were for you. One ounce is a handful.

Broccoli

Tell the kiddos they're eating brain food the next time you serve broccoli for dinner. This veggie is filled with antioxidants and plant compounds called carotenoids that are highly protective of the brain. I find even the pickiest eater likes it roasted.

Roasted Florets

1. Heat the oven to 425°.

2. Cut the florets from a stalk or two of broccoli and place them on a sheet pan protected with foil. Drizzle them with extra virgin olive oil, and sprinkle them with salt and pepper. Generously sprinkle on some garlic powder.

3. Place them on an upper rack in the oven, and let them roast until they are slightly burned around the edges.

Coffee

Don't ditch your java juice prematurely. Research confirms that coffee drinkers reduce their odds of developing Alzheimer's disease later in life. If what I just told you makes your heart beat with relief and joy, you may not be overthinking the issue. One of you is wondering, though, *just how does it do that?*

It is a stimulant and the notion that it keeps you up at night is true. Its molecular structure mimics adenosine, a neurotransmitter slowing your brain down at night. When caffeine binds with those same receptors, it doesn't slow down your brain, so you have more trouble falling asleep. I must confess that I love coffee so much, that I even enjoy a cup before bedtime with no ill effects at all. I must also admit that it's probably a matter of conditioning since I've enjoyed the habit for many years, but I love any diet that lets me drink all the coffee I want.

The bugaboo for me was not just the coffee flavors, but the creamer that made my coffee luscious. Flavored coffees are simply laboratory-derived additives included in the roasting process, so that burst my bubble right off the bat. Worse, I've never acquired the taste for strong black coffee. The sugar, corn syrup and dairy adds up and isn't part of a MIND diet, however, so I had to learn other ways to flavor my coffee, I went to the Coffee Detective. I began getting fresh beans, adding vanilla or ground pods of cinnamon to them before grinding them. For creamer, I learned to enjoy fat-free milk with a dash of vanilla and a touch of maple flavoring. Before long my taste buds caught up with my brain and all was well.

Aside from stimulation of the central nervous system and thus increasing alertness, does it really make for a healthier brain? The answer is, yes! Coffee contains antioxidants and its regular consumption is linked with a reduced rate of neurological diseases like Parkinson's and Alzheimer's. The evidence in your mind should be piling up. Antioxidants are vitally important to your brain.

Chapter Summary

We covered thirteen great brain foods. You got your first recipes for a happy, healthy brain.

- One of the most important things we covered is the importance of eating the right portions of these superfoods.

- Another important lesson was that there are ways to sneak these foods into the diets of picky eaters.

- A brain-healthy diet is multifaceted and contains a balance of these foods. Learn to like them all.

In the next chapter, you will learn which foods to subtract from your diet for better brain health. Don't let yourself have that reflex knee jerk reaction. It's not going to be that hard. I promise you, we'll get through this change together.

CHAPTER FOUR

FOODS YOUR BRAIN IS ADDICTED TO

Scientists rightfully classify heroin and opium as addictions, but they have been hesitant to add important new addictions to that category. One is **sugar**. According to Psychology Today, the average American eats 156 pounds of *added* sugar a year. About half comes from soft drinks, sporting energy drinks, and fruit drinks. That sugar triggers dopamine release in the brain's nucleus accumbens, the area associated with motivation, novelty, and reward. This is the same brain area that responds to cocaine and heroin. Think sugar cravings aren't an addictive response to your pleasure center? Think again.

These food addictions play a catch-22 with your brain, and ultimately with your life. Your brain's health requires removing them from your diet, but at the same time, your brain has become used to them and their addictive responses. It just keeps signaling for more. That's the power of an addiction. I replaced sugar for nine months with stevia-based substitutes and alcohol sugars. I not only saw the benefits in my waistline and joint health, (who knew sugar was such an inflammatory agent?), but I was more mentally alert. I became a believer in not just the present value of eating sugar-free but in the life-giving benefit of postponing a fate of dementia.

Mounting evidence suggests that diet plays a starring role in your brain health, and, no matter how overwhelmed you may be feeling about the topic right now, you can make these changes. Your goal is to stay away from anything that gives you brain fog and slows down the rhythm of brain productivity.

Research shows we can adapt to new lifestyles. You may have learned poor health habits growing up. You may have a lifetime of poor food choices behind you. That's okay. You *can* change. Found in the National Institute for the Clinical Application of Behavioral Medicine: "New research in neuroscience is showing that while our brains may have developed in a less than ideal manner, we can apply neuroplastic principles to help re-develop our brains." What does that mean in real language? It means you can train your brain to like and joyfully anticipate new foods.

What are the worst eight foods and how can you replace them with something brain healthy? Let me show you. If you just take favorites away you create a vacuum, and sooner or later your bad habits will return. The secret to change is in taking baby steps and then replacing an old favorite with a *new* favorite. My trek into the land of no sugar produced surprising health benefits, and I managed to keep cravings to a minimum. I'm not saying you can never enjoy special treats on special occasions. I'm encouraging you to find healthy replacements and occasionally treat yourself. I fall off the wagon during the holidays. I yield to temptation since I love pumpkin pie and Christmas cookies. Not just any pumpkin pie, but the old standby my mum used to make. Don't give me some doctored version when it's a holiday. *Don't mess with my holiday!* I want iced sugar cookies cut into Santas and stars, pumpkin pie with whipped cream, and all my favorite trimmings. After the holiday I climb back on the wagon and get back into the routine of charming my brain with clean eating all over again. See what I mean? It's not a life sentence. It's a matter of making peace with yourself as you make changes, give yourself grace, and putting lifelines into place.

That digression through the holidays takes place because I eat brain-healthy foods as a regular habit. It can only be a digression if you have a habit in the first place. How do you develop that habit?

Unsurprisingly, the trek into better eating habits begins with staying away from the middle shelves of the grocery aisles. Look at the top and bottom shelves. Many supermarkets now stock healthy alternatives in the same vicinity as the store: I find sugar free Lily baking chocolate in the same aisle as Hershey's. Learn to read labels. Begin a file of good-for-you recipes and a shopping list of items to replace your old standbys.

1 No-No: Commercial Muffins

Commercial bakeries still use hydrogenated oils, high fructose corn syrup, soybean oil, and trans fats. A study conducted in Montreal found that mice fed these substances displayed withdrawal symptoms when given a healthier diet. It's no secret that a muffin will probably give you a muffin top. A typical blueberry muffin (and blueberries are good for you, right?!) carries nearly 400 calories and a third of the day's fat. Yikes!

41

Remember we talked about eating clean? That means *eat the blueberries, not the muffin.* When you skip breakfast and find yourself tempted by a pastry at the coffee counter, opt for taking your coffee to your desk, where you've stashed some healthier options.

If you're at a meeting at Starbucks, that may not be an option. Just remember that a muffin with 500+ calories may be packing 25 grams of fat and 56 grams of **sugar** and 500 mg of sodium in the form of **salt**. A better alternative is a cheese Danish. It's still not perfect, but it's better, at half the levels of the muffin.

#2 No-No: Sugary Drinks, Including Sodas

There is absolutely nothing worthwhile about sodas or other sugary drinks. Aside from the quick sugar rush (followed by the inevitable sugar crash), you don't gain anything but added calories. Soda isn't the only culprit. Avoid energy drinks, sports drinks, and juices. *But orange juice is healthy, right?* Read the label and be sure there's no *added* sugar.

This is a hard habit to break, and some of you are already protesting that a zero-calorie soft drink can't be that bad for you. I'm sorry, but the research is not on your side. Forbes reported a study in the journal *Stroke,* which demonstrated a correlation between diet soda and both stroke and dementia. Those drinking at least one diet soda a day were three times as likely to develop dementia or suffer a stroke.

The best remedy is stopping soda cold turkey with a replacement of water. I know, it sounds harsh. A good step down might be having soda just with certain meals. When you splurge and have pizza, indulge in a soda. The rest of the time, refrain.

Focus on the healthy benefits of water. Did you know your body is 70% water and it needs up to 125 ounces a day, depending on who you read? What scientists do know is that the old advice of 64 fluid ounces is not the correct number. It's higher. Your brain needs a minimum of seven to eight *glasses, not cups,* a day for optimal brain health. Consider something as simple as sleeping through the night. You haven't lost sweat with exercise, but you are still waking up dehydrated. With each breath, water vapor is expired and your reserves are depleted.

Your inability to focus may be as simple as brain dehydration. You don't suspect dehydration when you're not crawling through the desert, but your brain needs water to concentrate. When you go into a fog it may be as simple as your brain conserving its resources.

The water you drink serves as a way to remove toxins from your brain. Your cerebral vessels need hydration to make those important cell transfers. The water you drink produces less concentrated blood, and thus it has more room for those toxins which built up when you were dehydrated when there was no room to transfer them out of the loading zone.

Obviously, water is good for you, but what if you just don't like it? Begin with adding infusions. They aren't expensive and they alter the flavor. You can also purchase powdery or liquid flavor enhancers, but be sure to read labels and avoid the ones with added sugar. Set a goal of how much water you want to drink per day or hour. Keep a water bottle handy. Get used to it. Water is your new best friend. Gradually decrease your need for flavorings and just drink the real deal. Your skin, your body, and your brain will thank you.

3 No-No: Canned Tuna

It's true that the American Heart Association recommends eating fatty fish like tuna at least twice a week, and sticking to their recommendation will be doing your brain a favor. Put canned tuna on the menu too often, however, and you could end up doing more harm than good. Why? Bigeye, ahi, albacore and yellowfin tuna are all high in mercury. Ingesting too much creates another set of concerns. Too much of the heavy metal can cause cognitive decline.

To stay on the safe side, incorporate other varieties of seafood like anchovies, wild salmon or trout. They offer the same benefits but don't carry the risk of excess mercury exposure. That's a little intimidating, isn't it? Salmon is very expensive and who likes anchovies?

I went on a rampage to learn to like them, and I discovered that sauteeing them in extra virgin olive oil, and then including just a few in other recipes changed my whole perspective. Pasta, spaghetti and pizza sauce all survived a little kick of anchovies without a storm of protests from my diners. I didn't simply eat anchovies or expect my family to. I started by using just the butter derived from searing them in olive oil and not the fish itself. I gradually added bits of fish as palates (mine included) got initiated to them. Not so bad! Better yet, they disappear into thin air when chopped up, so once you get used to the flavor, you'll never find them in a recipe where you've added them.

44

#4 No-No: Alcohol

Yes, some studies do promote one glass of wine per day, but overdoing it leads to lower cognitive function and lower overall brain health. A recent study of more than one million dementia patients in France found that one of the most preventable causes of dementia is alcohol consumption. In particular, the majority of early-onset dementia patients suffered from alcoholism or heavy drinking.

Learn to enjoy just a bit of wine paired with the entree of the meal. Resist the urge to indulge in mixed drinks or heavier forms of alcohol away from the dinner table.

#5 No-No: Refined Bread and Pasta

Refined bread and pastas have been stripped of their nutrients, so there remains no fiber to slow down metabolizing their nutrients. Instead, these processed carbohydrates rush through your system and cause a spike in blood sugar. A diet full of refined carbohydrates has been linked to impaired memory in both adults and children. This can be a hard one for bread lovers. (I particularly suffer when bread is removed from the diet.)

I'm not a fan of many of the whole grain alternatives, either. My transition to healthier eating was the implementation of a step-down program. I was strict with myself and kept track of meals. In the first week, for every five meals of yummy pasta or crusty french bread, I ate one with whole grains. In the second week, I dropped it to 4:1, and then 3:1, etc. I held at a 2:1 ratio. For every two meals with refined carbohydrates, I substitute one with whole grains *in the same food.*

For example, I like wild rice. I also like white french bread. Wild rice isn't my substitute for refined bread. Wild rice is a substitute for refined white rice. Homemade whole-grain biscuits are my substitute for French bread. See what I mean? Whenever possible I substitute brown or wild rice for white rice. I keep whole wheat flour on hand as well.

My Doctored Whole Wheat Biscuit Recipe

Preheat the oven to 450°.

Combine 2 cups whole wheat flour with some special seasonings: ½ tsp salt, ½ tsp ground mustard, ½ tsp sage, and ½ tsp celery seed. Add 4 teaspoons of baking powder.

Cut in a half stick of hard butter. Work it gently and just to pea-sized pieces.

Pour in 1 cup of sour milk. (I add a dash of lemon juice or apple cider vinegar to fresh milk to make it sour.)

Work your dough and form it on a floured surface into a slab about an inch thick. Cut out biscuits and bake for ten to twelve minutes.

These savory biscuits are crowd-pleasers, and I sometimes have to make four or five batches when there's a holiday full house.

#5 No-No: Soy Sauce

It doesn't seem like a big deal sprinkled on your sushi, but just one tablespoon has nearly 40% of your daily **salt** recommendation. What has salt got to do with a foggy brain? A lot, actually. According to a Hypertension journal study, highly concentrated sodium-packed foods can restrict blood vessels and thereby impair focus, organizational skills, and memory. High salt intake can also cause an electrolyte imbalance with resultant dehydration, making it difficult to keep your head in the game.

The next time you order sushi, opt for a low-sodium soy sauce or eel sauce (which tastes a lot like teriyaki) and keep the serving size small. Making this simple swap can cut your sodium intake in half, keeping your focus laser-sharp.

#6 No-No: Vegetable Oils

It only *sounds* like they're healthy. You might be thinking vegetable oils have got to be better for you than butter, but don't bet on it. You'd be wrong. Certain oils, like sunflower, soybean and canola oil do have higher levels of omega-6 antioxidants. But this fatty acid causes inflammation in the brain. What you want are omega-3 fatty acids.

A better choice is extra virgin olive oil. You can use it anywhere when you would have used butter, including over vegetables, in baked goods, and even on popcorn!

#7 No-No: Too Much Red Meat

Some red meat is good for you, but if that sounds like permission to have beef every other night, you'd be wrong. Studies have shown a correlation between populations that eat diets high in red meat and the increased incidence of Alzheimer's disease. One plausible theory is that it raises iron levels in the bloodstream, and iron causes oxidative damage. The sad result of cell deterioration and brain damage doesn't make that burger or steak quite as palatable, does it?

★ When you do buy meat at the supermarket, look for grass-fed cuts, and limit the nights you serve beef.

Chapter Summary

Are you still with me? Remember, it's baby steps with all of these treasured favorites. Reduce the no-nos and slowly implement changes. You can do this. Find friends with similar values and start a supper club. You'll learn new recipes and get a lot of moral support.

• You learned the fallacy of canned tuna as a primary way to increase fatty fish consumption.

• You learned a dynamite new recipe for whole-grain biscuits. That's a win!

• You learned the one thing that sounds the hardest. It's different for every person, but you know what you dread losing from your line up. That's your challenge. Begin chipping away at bad habits. Coach John says, "Baby steps," right?

In the next chapter, you will learn just how easy it is to craft a brain-healthy menu.

CHAPTER FIVE

THE MIND DIET IMPROVES BRAIN HEALTH

We eat for all kinds of reasons, don't we? Some people eat for bodybuilding. They want to enter competitions where they grease their bodies and lift weights. By eating certain foods in certain ways, they optimize their program. Some people eat for their waistlines. They want to look a certain way, so they diet and watch their food intake. Some people eat for their hearts. They've been scared by a cardiac incident, and they change the way they eat for heart health. Watching what you eat is not a new thing in any way, shape or form.

But eating brain food, a diet specifically designed to enhance your thinking and cognitive function, may still seem radical to you. Let me remind you why you're doing this: you want to improve your function. That means you must feed your brain what *it wants to eat*. Yup, my friend, it's that simple. Your brain functions at peak levels when it receives the nourishment it craves, and that means tweaking your diet.

I referred to dietary studies earlier in this book and demonstrated the data and the statistics behind their efficacy. As your coach, I want to encourage you to take this next step. Hopefully, you practiced the recipes in the last chapter. They are meant to whet your whistle, so to speak, to show you that you *can happily* make these changes. Let's make a pact with one another, shall we?

Try this plan for sixty days. *Whoa! That's quite a commitment!* I can hear what you're thinking and you're coming in loud and clear. The twenty-one days to form a new habit is an urban legend. You heard me right. It's a myth. Not true. A lie.

It stems from an audiobook written by a plastic surgeon who looked at the way patients became accustomed to a new appearance after reconstructive surgery. He found it took them about twenty-one days to get accustomed to their new appearances. From that, it became popular to assume it took twenty-one days to form a new habit. It's easy. Anyone can try something for twenty-one days, right? Sadly, it left many unhappy with the outcome and feeling rather inadequate. They tried. The new habit just didn't stick.

New research explains just why. A study published in the European Journal of Social Psychology demonstrated that it took an average of sixty-six days to form a new habit. For many, it took three months. The study was based on a twelve-week longitudinal study of self-reporting behaviors and illustrated the reason why a longer trial is needed than three weeks. *We all slip off the wagon upon occasion.* During the eighty-four days of the study, missing one day had no effect on the outcome of the trial. New habits were formed. Expanding the effort compensated for the off day we normally experience upon occasion. Make no mistake. It takes time to change. and then keep the change.

It's true. Therapists and coaches across all disciplines now forecast ninety days to ameliorate an addictive behavior, and there's nothing more addictive than food. None of us can live without it, and it's a behavior we indulge in regularly. I'm not going to sugarcoat the facts. Remember, I promised *not to lie to you!*

So here's Coach John talking. Create a chart or purchase a planner with a calendar in it. I'm not asking you to measure calories or record your diet, though you may find it beneficial. *I am asking you to track your progress. Self-evaluate each day if you followed the plan.* Do this for three months. Then look back over the experiment and evaluate your performance. I am providing you with both recipes and meal plans in the back of this book. If you want to do this the easy way, just follow my ninety days of meal plans. If you are the creative or adventurous sort, take the recipes you love and create your own.

Most of my successful partners begin with the meal plan, and soon cross over to planning their own diets. They get the knack of what is being suggested and find it easy to adapt. I think you'll be like most of my partners. That's why I'm describing the plan in detail for you. Understand it. Follow my suggestions for a week or two, and then leap out on your own. Don't worry right now about digression from the plan. I'll cover how to eat at a restaurant or party without derailing your success as we go along. For right now, just understand the science behind the MIND dietary regimen and don't freak out, okay? Still with me?

Let's begin. Eating certain foods (and avoiding others) has been shown to slow brain aging by 7.5 years, and lessen the chances of developing Alzheimer's disease. It's called the MIND diet, derived from a study funded by the National Institute on Aging and conducted at the Rush University Medical Center. Nutritional epidemiologist Martha Clare Morris, Ph.D., blended the popular DASH (Dietary Approaches to Stop Hypertension) diet, and the Mediterranean diet, into a hybrid regimen emphasizing foods proven to impact brain health.

Why is it so helpful? Because it removes the necessity to prepare full menus by a meal plan. True, I'm providing the meticulous-of-mind an outline to follow, but here's the key point: *You don't need to make it hard. It's meant to be an easy guideline for healthy living.* Say *yes* to some things. Say *No* to others. Yup. It's just that simple.

Here's what it looks like, pared down to essentials. You're going to love how easy it is to eat a brain-healthy diet!

Load your plate with certain vegetables

As it turns out, your mother was right all along. Clean your plate and eat your veggies. Dark green leafy vegetables are specifically shown to lower the risk of dementia and cognitive decline. I know some of you are dying to ask: Why?

I'll tell you. Greens are packed with nutrients linked to better brain health, nutrients like folate, vitamin E, carotenoids and flavonoids. Just one serving a day has been shown to slow brain aging. That's *one serving*. Expand that for optimal success. To jazz up your diet, aim to

52

eat at least six servings a week of greens. Then round it out with at least one serving of another vegetable each day.

Eat berries for dessert

I suppose you're familiar with the saying, *An apple a day keeps the doctor away.* I try to eat one each day, myself. But when scientists reviewed the studies on diet and brain health, one type of fruit proved more significant than all the rest. In a twenty-year study of over 16,000 older adults, those who ate the most blueberries and strawberries had the slowest rates of cognitive decline. Researchers credit the high levels of flavonoids in berries with the benefit.

Treat yourself to two or more berry servings a week for peak brain health. Remember we talked about clean eating earlier in the book? Yes. Just eat berries. Cut down your time in the kitchen and *just eat the berries.* The USDA sets serving portions for most fruits and vegetables, and you may be wondering by now, what constitutes a serving? It's easier to picture a serving size of kale or spinach prepared in a salad or side dish, but berries standing alone as your dessert are a little harder to fathom. They suggest one cup, but really? That's eight large strawberries. Just 2.6 ounces of blueberries is about half a cup. So figure on half a pint of blueberries.

Snack on nuts (and pass on the Oreos)

Nuts, as we have discussed, are high in calories and fat, but they are also loaded with fat-soluble vitamin E. We've talked about vitamin E more than once, so by now you recognize how much your brain appreciates its stellar qualities. It's a good trade-off. Grab a handful of

53

brain-healthy nuts at least five times a week. Skip the processed snacks like chips or pastries, and that means foregoing the Oreos. Be a label reader. Check the list of ingredients, and opt for dry-roasted or raw, unsalted varieties to avoid the extra sodium sweeteners or oils. Just as a caveat, be aware that no-stir peanut butter usually have stuff added in. You can find healthy varieties, but *read the labels*!

Cook much of the time with extra virgin olive oil

Another Mediterranean diet staple you'll see in the MIND diet is extra virgin olive oil. Researchers recommend avoiding butter and margarine. Use more olive oil. That was a steep change for our household. We were among the original Mrs. Buttertons, and that was a hard habit to break. Here's what we discovered: Cooking with olive oil and seasoning with fresh herbs made our favorite dishes just as palatable. Growing windowsill herbs was a treat for both the eye and the stomach.

New to olive oil? Rachael Ray coined the popular EVOO, extra-virgin olive oil, and that's exactly what you're looking for on the label. If you'll remember from earlier in the book, extra virgin relates to the way it has been processed, without chemicals. Further, purchase a bottle in opaque or darkened glass to preserve its integrity and freshness.

Learn to enjoy meat-free meals

Brain-healthy eating encourages means you will start to eat less meat. Count on eating red meat less than four times a week in the ideal MIND diet. Beans, lentils and soybeans, all rich in protein and fiber, make a worthy substitute. They offer satiety, and, as an added benefit, are rich in B vitamins, also very important in brain health. I have not one, but two dog-eared copies of *Diet for a Small Planet*. Lappe offers evidence and recipes on how to begin changing out meat-laden menus for healthier alternatives.

I eventually lost or loaned out my first copy and had to purchase a second. Naturally, I found my original, so now I have two, and I'm able to loan one out at will. Ms. Lappe talks a lot about complementary proteins, and I'll share how I've adapted some of the recipes and created my favorites in the back of the book. For now, just roll the concept over and over in your brain. Get used to the sound of it. I promise you, it's not as painful as it sounds.

Plan on fish once a week

Do you have trouble remembering the names of people you just met? It's common as we age...or is it? Adults (over the age of 65) who reported eating fish once a week earned higher scores on memory tests than their counterparts who didn't like fish. That's right. They remembered facts better and did better in number games than the non-fish eaters. If you are not a fan of fish, take heart: there is no evidence than eating it more than once a week offers any extra benefit for your brain.

That's once a week for peak performance. You got this, right?

It's okay to drink wine

Obviously, I'm not talking about over-indulgence. Too much alcohol is bad for your body on so many levels. However, studies do suggest that a glass of wine in moderation may lower your risk of dementia. I mean, it may delay the onset of Alzheimer's disease by one to two years. That's pretty significant.

Look back through your planners for the last two years. What significant events would you have missed if your brain checked out too early? Weddings, holidays, promotions, graduations, many special events dot your life. They are significant for you, and also significant for your family and friends. Be good to yourself and your loved ones. Guard your brain so you can continue to enjoy those events!

Chapter Summary

We covered a lot of key foods in this chapter, foods you need to include in your diet.

- Eat more green, leafy vegetables.

- Try clean eating your sweet treats.

- Be a nut (by eating more nuts).

- Opt for extra virgin olive oil.

- Eat less meat.

- Eat more fish.

- Have a cup of wine with your dinner.

In the next chapter, we are going to roll up our sleeves and deep dive into the meal plans that will optimize your brain health. I'm excited!

CHAPTER SIX

WHAT'S ON YOUR GROCERY LIST?

Theory alone doesn't get it done. If you really want to protect your brain, it's time to put it into practice. We can learn all we want and say all the right buzzwords. Until we dig in and make it happen, it's just that. Talk. It's time to get down to business and go from dabbling with the idea to seeing what a day on the MIND diet looks like. You'll want to read through it, try it and get used to it. We talked about trying it for three months, and this is your first taste of what a day in the MIND diet looks and tastes and feels like...I hope you enjoy it!

Let's review. The MIND diet means:

- Six servings a week of green, leafy veggies, and one serving a day of other vegetables

- Five servings of nuts a week.

- Two servings of berries each week.

- Three servings of beans and legumes a week.

- Down with the red meat, up with the white--two servings of poultry a week.

- Get fishy with your menu once a week.

- Ditch the butter, cook with olive oil.

- Enjoy one glass of wine a day.

Being specific, your no-nos include cutting red meat to less than four servings a week, cutting butter to less than one tablespoon a day, reducing cheese to less than one serving a week, holding pastries and sweets down to less than five servings a week, and indulging in fast food less than once a week. These are your starting parameters. Work at reducing them as your ninety-day trial moves forward.

Breakfast

No one questions the role of breakfast for good health, so it's a no-brainer than your brain loves breakfast as well. This was a tricky one for me. My usual hunger alarm sounds off around 10:00 am, despite my need to be out the door by 7:30 in the morning. My formerly bad habit of staying up late, and sleeping until the last possible minute, further complicated the process of eating a healthy and nutritious breakfast.

Making the switch to a MIND breakfast required a complete paradigm shift for me and by extension, my family. We talked about it. We mapped out what a week of MIND breakfasts looked like, and then hit the grocery store. We started with the goal of having a MIND breakfast twice that first week, and then broadened our menus and gradually increased it. Here's our first effort in making that transition.

Start your day with a brain-boosting breakfast. Eat a whole-grain cereal, and we found we appreciated steel-cut oats, topping them with nuts and berries. It was easier for us to start it the night before in a crockpot, and then we added the toppings in the morning. This was our first effort. It's a great dump recipe, and it's easy to make.

Apple Pie Oatmeal

Serves two.

Dump two sliced apples into a crockpot.

Add ⅓ cup stevia sugar. We used brown sugar.

1 tsp cinnamon

Dump two cups of steel-cut oats on top.

Pour 4 cups of water over the top.

Do not stir. Cook overnight for eight to nine hours. In the morning, top each bowl with a handful of nuts and ½ to 1 cup of blueberries. We dribbled a little fat-free milk on top and chowed down.

It helped that we started in the fall when crisp mornings began the order of the day. It was warm, rib-sticking and such a delight. Before long it became a weekly staple the whole family enjoyed.

Lunch

Lunch for me was often a desk affair. I developed the bad habit of grabbing fast food and dashing back to my desk to eat it while I worked. It's no wonder my brain got sluggish by mid-afternoon, leading to a Snickers to get me through the rest of the day. This meal was pivotal for me in changing over to a brain-healthy way of eating.

★ The key was in making a great evening meal in portions large enough to allow for leftovers to bring to work. The break room microwave heated my meal and I ate at the desk as I worked, the same as always.

More importantly, I no longer experienced the usual 3:00 pm slump. I was a working machine all afternoon.

Mid-Afternoon Snack

At first, I kept containers of nuts and trail mix (minus the M & Ms) at my desk to nibble on and ease cravings on the days when I *didn't* have a brain-healthy lunch. Since I love nuts, this was easy. I eventually developed a pattern for my snack foods, but more on that in the next chapter!

Dinner

The majority of my calories and fats were traditionally eaten during dinner. I needed dementia-fighting recipes, and, at first, shunned the idea of trying new foods like quinoa. I grew up as a meat and potatoes kind of guy, suspicious of new ingredients. My adventurous spirit was a developing thing, once I got used to feeling good and wanting to put some variety into my life.

Swashbuckling Clucker

Serves 6

We had to be creative to bring the whole family along on this endeavor, and it meant adapting recipes and coming up with more attractive names for the meals. Don't ask me how we arrived at this moniker for a Mediterranean style of pasta. I think our children were into pirates and we used sabers (long knives) to slice ingredients. But do you see how easy it is to lure little minds (mine included!) into the adventure of exploring a whole new way of eating? This was our first foray into the world of healthy, brain-loving MIND dinners.

Boil lightly salted water and cook a package of whole-grain pasta al dente. Rinse it.

Prepare for stir fry:

- 2 chicken breasts, sliced thin or cubed

- 1 onion, minced

- 4 cups washed spinach, sliced into narrow ribbons the younguns' can't pick out

- 1 package mushrooms, cleaned with a damp paper towel, sliced

- 1 clove of minced garlic

- 1 cup of sliced almonds

- a handful of minced herbs

Sautee the stir fry ingredients in extra-virgin olive oil in the order given. When they are ready, add your bow-tie pasta. We topped it with chopped fresh herbs since we had window sill pots of sage, basil, rosemary, and flat-leaf parsley. Our favorite on this was the flat-leaf parsley. Then we dribbled on a little more olive oil to make sure it was moist.

This became a favorite of everyone in the family. Our household heartily recommends it.

Your Shopping List

For week one, pick up these items at the grocery store:

From the fresh aisle:

1 container of steel-cut oats

2 pints of blueberries

a bag of apples

1 eight-ounce container of fresh mushrooms

1 large bag of fresh spinach

1 small onion

1 bulb of garlic

1 small bundle of fresh herbs if you're ready to pack some flavor into your meal

From the grocery aisles:

1 tub of steel-cut oats

a sugar substitute. We use both stevia and sugar alcohol substitutes.

a large sack of sliced almonds from the bulk canisters

one package of whole-grain bow tie pasta

one bottle of extra-virgin olive oil

From the meat counter:

2 chicken breasts

From the dairy aisle:

1 gallon fat-free milk

Are you ready? Be brave. Give it a try. You are armed with all the facts, and you know the benefits. Now you have a plan to try out. This is where the rubber meets the road. This is where you invest some effort and get ready to chart your progress.

★ Remember we talked about that chart? Put a star or checkmark on each square where you inserted a MIND meal into your daily routine. Snacks count, of course. Your goal by day 90 is to have three or four marks of valor in each square. This is how you measure your progress in a visual way that reinforces your efforts.

Chapter Summary

Reading about brain health does little good when you aren't *eating* brain-healthy foods. It's time to invest a little effort and money into learning how to live for a dementia-free future.

• Remember, we're only trying it out this week. It's one day. Twenty-four hours.

• These are baby steps. Trying too much too soon is a form of self-sabotage.

• You have everything you need to be successful at this, all you need is to show up at the table.

In the next chapter, you will learn how to snack healthy. This is just as important as your first-day trial run.

CHAPTER SEVEN

THE BEST BRAIN FOODS FOR SNACKING. PERIOD.

Let's face it. Sometimes you're going to snack. Whether it's the big game, cramming for a test, finishing a project, or just vegging with friends, you're going to snack. Some of your current snacks aren't helping. Sugary snacks lead to a sugar crash followed by an emergency nap. Salty chips and artery-clogging dips are just downright unhealthy. The right snacks will make you more productive. Eat things to sharpen your focus. Nibble on brain foods.

Let's focus on good snacks. Good appetizers. Foods you, your family, your guests will enjoy. I'll start with snacks you can use to stock the pantry, ever available for a quick pick-me-up, and then add recipes for items you'll want to prepare for that special event.

- ❖ Go nuts for nuts. Almonds are healthy and enjoyable. If you're not a fan, try peanuts, cashews, walnuts or pistachios.

- ★ The trick here is to purchase the unsalted varieties and sprinkle on just the amount you want.

- ❖ Unseeded grapes. Pick up a bunch when they're on sale, pop them into a ziplock bag and toss them into the freezer.

★ If you have children, you may need to hide them. Ours found the stash and grabbed some to take outside. Let's face it. They grabbed the whole baggie and absconded with their loot!

❖ Dark chocolate. You'll no doubt remember all of the benefits (antioxidants and natural stimulants) for your brain. Think about the endorphins and happy thoughts you're providing at the same time. Also, remember the calories. This is a nibbling snack, not a grazing commodity.

❖ Air-popped popcorn. Make a healthy version, dribbling on some extra virgin olive oil, and then sprinkling on some salt. Keep a shaker of cinnamon sugar handy if you've got sweets on the brain. Make it healthy and enjoy it because it's a snack.

★ Ditch those microwave bags and get used to popping your own.

❖ Veggies and hummus. You know you like it, but did you know it's good for you? Made with chickpeas, it's high in B vitamins and the fiber is rib-sticking.

★ When you buy your veggies, don't just plop them in your fridge as you put your groceries away. Take a few moments to wash and slice them for easy snacking. You'll find it much easier to turn to a healthy snack if it's ready and waiting.

❖ Greek Yogurt. Not only is it higher in protein (twice as much per serving), it's chock-full of bone-building nutrients and gut-happy probiotics as well.

★ Ditch those sugary varieties and season your own. Drizzle in honey or add some leftover fruit salad.

★ Jazz it up for company as a fruit parfait. I use clear plastic cups to appreciate its full effect. Alternate layers of yogurt with layers of fresh fruits and top it off with a few flakes of oatmeal. This is company-ready to impress guests or treat your family on a sleepy Saturday morning.

❖ Trail mix. Keep it in an air-tight container for up to a month, so it's always available in a pinch. Be wary of store-bought varieties, made with hydrogenated oil, salt, and sugar.

★ Make your own. Use pumpkin seeds, cashews, sunflower seeds, pecans, almonds, dried cranberries, raisins...but skip the candy. Replace it with luxuries like dried pineapple or other favorite yummies.

❖ Fruit salad. Make a big batch and use it for breakfast as well as snacks. Use all your favorite fruits, like apples, oranges, grapes, strawberries, blueberries, kiwi, unsweetened pineapple chunks and bananas. Besides satisfying the taste buds, you'll be filling your body with good energy, natural fiber and a host of vitamins and minerals.

★ We love a handful of chopped mint in ours. Keep some on your windowsill and it will always be in season.

❖ If you can't resist the urge to dip, dip apples in peanut butter. Yum!

★ If you're making them for a party, fashion those delightful little sandwiches you can find on Pinterest.

❖ Roasted chickpeas. If you need to find the perfect alternative to chips or crackers, you've found it. It's full of fiber and protein.

★ Roast them in the oven at 200° for 45 minutes to an hour. Season them with chili powder and a dash of salt. For a variety, add garlic and parmesan or honey and cinnamon.

❖ Avocado anything. We love to mash it up and spread it on toast. Make guacamole and please everyone!

❖ Banana ice yum. Treat yourself to your daily dose of potassium by buying bunches on sale. Peel and freeze them for smoothies, or just whip them in your food processor for a creamy ice cream substitute.

❖ Kale chips. Yup. Roast them like chickpeas and nosh on them in place of potato chips.

No chapter like this would be complete without a section on smoothies. These are the ultimate go-tos for our family. Most of our creations begin with ice. Toss in your fruit. Add your seasonings. I generally toss in a handful of frozen kale. (They never notice it.) Pour in a little almond milk or water or juice. Set your blender to smoothie and get those taste buds ready. You may need to stop it if frozen fruit gets lodged in the bottom. (You'll know it needs a nudge because your blender will start groaning and ultimately smoking.) I use a wooden spoon handle to smoosh it around and add a dash more liquid. Then it's

68

humming on all four cylinders. I add one or two packets of stevia if it taste tests on the tart side. I always have some non-sugary protein powder on hand if my jeans feel tight and I need a keto snack. I have a tall glass that's always brimming with straws for any occasion. These are our favorite versions! You'll notice I seldom measure anything. Let's make this simple and easy.

- ❖ Chocolate Yum. A few ice cubes, frozen bananas, a couple of tablespoons of peanut butter, frozen kale, a quarter cup of oatmeal flakes and a heaping spoonful of cocoa. Sometimes I throw in a smidge of almond milk.

- ❖ Blueberry Delight. Start with a few ice cubes, add some frozen bananas, of course. Add one of those sacks of frozen blueberries you got on sale and stashed away for future use. I usually add some almond milk.

- ❖ Choco-Avi-Shake. Half an avocado, a few tablespoons cocoa, one or two packets of stevia, a teaspoon of vanilla, a cup of ice and some coconut milk. Yum! Deeply satisfying and keto to boot!

- ❖ Aloha Smoothie. Oranges and pineapple pieces with fruit juice.

- ❖ Sunshine Shake. Strawberries and bananas, vanilla protein powder with almond milk.

- ❖ Choco-Berry. A few ice cubes, fresh or frozen strawberries, a couple of tablespoons of cocoa, some frozen kale and almond milk.

❖ Tummy Trimmer. A banana, a handful of oats, a handful of frozen strawberries, and a cup or so of water.

❖ Chocolate Frostie. Ice cubes, a couple of tablespoons of cocoa powder, a small frozen banana, a half teaspoon of vanilla, a pint of almond milk. (Frozen kale just makes it look more chocolatey.)

❖ It's a Date. I use almond butter instead of peanut butter. Chop up a couple of pitted dates, add a banana, and a cup of almond milk.

❖ Green, Green, Green. Of course, it's almost pure spinach. I add either a sliced apple or pieces of pineapple. I always have a frozen banana in the freezer. Sometimes I toss in some leftover cucumber. I include a couple of tablespoons of plain greek yogurt. Top it off with some orange juice. This is a detoxifying smoothie that won't hurt your tastebuds.

Dress up your smoothies with a garnish of fruit, or line a ring of some sliced bananas around a clear glass. Sprinkle some oats on the top. These are worthy of any occasion from a weekend breakfast to a summer afternoon pick-me-up. They make a great breakfast on the go, rinsing out your plastic glass once you hit the office.

Appetizers occupy a fair amount of my attention. From company parties to neighborhood socials to having a crowd over for the game, sometimes I just need something fancier than Ants on a Log (celery with peanut butter topped with raisins). The worst part is I always seem to need an appetizer on my busiest day of the week when I am the least prepared and most frazzled. That's why you need a few go-to ideas, so you're never tempted to relapse into the chips and dip mode (Gasp! Don't do it!) These appetizers are sure to please, and I've only included those recipes of things you can make from a well-stocked cupboard or freezer.

★ There's a grocery list at the end of this chapter. Stock up. Prepare the veggies or fruits as directed as you unpack and store them. It will make life easier, and you'll never be scratching your head feeling like a dunce.

Being prepared is the antidote to serving your friends and family something that looks good, but is filled with unwanted, artery-clogging fat. They don't have to be fried or topped with mounds of cheese. Adapt to a healthier style of entertaining and don't sacrifice class in the process. I promise you, these are pleasing to the eye, mouth-watering, and dare I say it? Let me whisper it. *Healthy*. Opt for quality. Always. Here are a few of our favorites.

Poseidon's Spear

These are incredibly simple, glamorous. They join crunch with savory yumminess. And yes, you can prepare them in minutes.

1. Score the skin on an English cucumber, leaving a few pieces for color. Slice the cucumber.

2. Top each slice with a dollop of Greek yogurt seasoned with dill and horseradish. (I use a ratio of 3:1 when mixing it up. One cup

of yogurt with three tablespoons of dill and one tablespoon of horseradish.

3. Lay some bite-sized pieces of smoked salmon on top.

4. Now spear it all with a fancy cocktail pick.

5. Lay some leftover dill sprigs in the tray and voila! It's ready for sampling.

Plated Apples

These are certain winners (if you're competitive, which I'm not, laughing hard here). Pairing the sweet crunch of apple with the savory flavor of chicken salad is genius! Pure genius.

1. I always buy a couple of rotisserie chickens when they are on sale. I debone them, chop the chicken, and freeze them in labeled ziplock bags. The messy step is done when it's time to make an appetizer. Pull one out of the freezer and zap it in the microwave for a minute, and you're good to go.

2. Turn that thawed chicken into a bowl. Add dried cranberries, roasted chopped pecans, thin-sliced celery, halved grapes, small bits of pineapple, etc. If you haven't figured it out yet, I just empty the refrigerator of whatever I have on hand. You can't mess this up. Seriously.

3. Create a dressing. I start with Greek yogurt, and add some lemon juice, salt and pepper, a dash of curry powder.

4. Slice a whole apple into thin little plates. If you aren't using this immediately, splash the apple in a slurry of lemon juice so it doesn't turn brown.

5. Put a spoon of chicken salad on each of the plates. Boom!

6. Pair them with a white wine and you've just taken it from game food to parlor foot in one easy step.

Pinwheels

I don't care what day of the week it is, there's always a bag of tortillas in my fridge. We love tacos and burritos, and these take the place of bread in sandwiches. What great vehicles for getting the filling to the mouth with clean fingers and happy tummies for the score! These plate up nicely and make a great presentation.

1. Start with any flavored tortilla you have on hand.

2. Create the spread by mixing in a bowl hummus, chopped spinach, chopped basil, some sun-dried tomatoes, and stir in a few toasted pine nuts.

3. Slather each tortilla with a layer of your mix, and roll them up.

4. Slice and plate them. Add a sprig of fresh herbs for a garnish to make the dish extra fancy.

Not Your Mother's Stuffed Mushrooms

These are pretty fancy-shmancy! The best part is, you won't need to sacrifice flavor for empty calories. This taking brain food to a whole new level. Think of it this way: Start with fiber and lots of vitamins and minerals. Add a whole lot of antioxidants. Season with sprinkles of flavor. Pop them in the oven, and, in minutes, you have something fabulous to serve at even the fanciest of occasions. They are perfectly sized, super cute, and oh so good for you.

1. Preheat your oven to 350°.

2. Wipe fresh mushrooms with a damp cloth. Remove the stems. I make a couple of dozen because they disappear so quickly. Lay them on a baking sheet.

3. Mix up a bowl of yummy stuffing:

   a. I use a base of leftover quinoa, about a half cup.

   b. Add two or three minced cloves of garlic. If your family likes it, add a quarter cup of chopped onion. Saute this in some extra virgin olive oil.

   c. Use a couple of handfuls of chopped spinach, and add it to the pan. I usually add my leftover quinoa here, to warm it up.

   d. Throw in some chopped pecans.

   e. Chop up the mushroom stems and add them. Let's not waste anything.

   f. I often season the mix with a couple of tablespoons of parmesan cheese from the fridge,

4. Fill the mushrooms, mounding up your luscious stuffing.

5. Bake them for fifteen or twenty minutes.

6. Plate them and pair your appetizer with a glass of white wine to make it a black-tie affair.

Mama Mia Sweet Peppers

These sweet peppers come in several colors rich in antioxidants, Vitamin B$_6$, Vitamins C and A. They are full of fiber, and you never even need to slice or dice them and you may ignore the mess with their seeds. There's nothing easier than this! Marinate the peppers and serve them. Did I mention this was a speedy appetizer? Keep them in a sealed canning jar for a lovely presentation, and you'll have the kiddos begging to fish them out.

1. Buy sweet peppers in those two pound bags.

2. Wash and dry them.

3. Coat them with some extra virgin olive oil, and char them in an oven set to about 325°; turn them after about five minutes, charring both sides. Let them cool.

4. Chop equal amounts of herbs. I usually use dill and parsley because I always have some in the windowsill. Dice them up and get them ready.

5. Prepare the marinade:

    a. Add about six packets of stevia.

    b. You'll need to put in a crazy amount of salt. Don't flinch. Just add two tablespoons of salt. Remember, they will be sitting in it, and you aren't drinking it.

    c. Stir in a cup of white vinegar and water.

    d. Put herbs in the bottom of a sealing jar. Pack in the roasted peppers, Pour on the marinade. Let the peppers soak up the flavor overnight, and serve them straight from the jar with a long fork for spearing them and pulling them out.

Buffalo Bites (aka Not Your Normal Chicken Wings)

Sometimes you just need them. No judging here. We make these minus the chicken, and calorie-conscious guests never complain. They are fiber-filled and great for dipping. You'll need napkins. These are crazy good and if you can live without the chicken, much better for you.

1. Preheat the oven to a hot 450°. Spray it with a non-stick coating and have it ready.

2. Break up cauliflower florets and toss them into this coating mixture:

   a. ½ cup flour

   b. Add your favorite seasonings. We like a teaspoon of garlic powder, salt and pepper. Stir them together.

   c. Add ½ cup water.

3. Place your coated cauliflower onto your prepared baking sheet and give them about fifteen minutes. You will probably need to flip them once in the process.

4. Remove them when they are ready, but leave the oven on for the next step. Drizzle on some extra virgin olive oil and toss the cauliflower florets to coat them. Put them back on the baking sheet and continue baking them for another half hour. You want them crispy.

5. When you take them from the oven, allow them a resting period of ten or fifteen minutes.

6. Serve them with a dipping sauce of plain Greek yogurt mixed with garlic powder and chopped dill.

Salsa Addiction

We can't get enough of this, and we make an enormous batch. Serve it with baked pita rounds for a healthier version of chips and salsa. It's good on any grilled chicken or fish. It dressed up celery sticks. You can't go wrong with it in any combination. It's the perfect date for any party. I use mostly fresh ingredients, mix it up in the bowl and it's done.

4 chopped tomatoes. You can get fussy and use Romas, but I use what I have.

1 medium mango, peeled and chopped. I usually chop them on the pit.

1 ripe, chopped avocado

¾ to one cup of thawed frozen corn

1 can of drained, washed black beans

1 small red onion, diced finely

2 or 3 diced cloves of garlic

Diced jalapenos. If I take the seeds out, I use four. I leave the seeds in, I use two. Wear gloves for this process and for heaven's sake, don't rub your eye. (Been there, done that.)

1 bunch of diced cilantro

3 tablespoons lime juice

1 tablespoon extra virgin olive oil

Grocery List

Did you see what was missing from all these appetizers and smoothies and people pleasers? Red meat. I used one rotisserie chicken from my freezer. You're going to start revising the way you buy groceries, and instead of spending way too much money on red meat, allocate a few of those saved dollars to the fresh produce aisle. I'm giving you a list of items I keep on stock. Some I use as appetizers, and whatever isn't in a recipe or salad gets included on a plate of fresh veggies.

I also deal with my produce when I bring it into the kitchen. Life gets hectic and having the prep work done makes a huge difference. I know, it's a matter of switching one time slot to another, but trust me. When your fresh produce is prepped and ready for use, it won't go to waste. You will use it.

Produce

- apples, 1 bag

- oranges, 1 bag

- red onions

- sweet baby peppers

- celery--break apart stalks, clean them, cut them into sections you will use

- carrots--peel them, cut them into strips

- bananas--buy 4 or 5 bunches, peel, and freeze most of them in sandwich baggies stowed inside freezer bags.

- fresh spinach--I wash and bag portions. If I can't use it fast enough, I freeze it for smoothies to replace ice cubes.)

- nuts and seeds (We typically buy them in bulk at the produce section.)

- garlic, 1 head or bulb

- avocados if you will be using them

- English cucumber (with an edible skin)--slice them

- head of cauliflower (or 2)--Remove the florets and keep them in a baggie in the fridge

- blueberries, 1 or 2 pints. Clean and freeze ½ cup to a sandwich baggie stored in freezer bags

- strawberries--unless you're using them the next day, process them. Clean, cut off the stems, slice and freeze in portioned sandwich baggies, stowing several in larger freezer bags

- seedless grapes, whatever's on sale

- mango if you're making salsa

- jalapenos if you're making salsa

- tomatoes

- pineapple if it's on sale--peel, cut and freeze bite-sized sections

- mushrooms if they are on sale and you are stuffing them this week

- dried cranberries, and other dried fruits if you're making trail mix

- fresh herbs if you don't have a windowsill garden

Grocery Goods

- cans of black beans when they are on sale

- quinoa

- spices

- 75-80% dark cocoa

- cans of sun-dried tomatoes

- pita bites if you're needing a vehicle for carrying a yummy morsel

- peanut butter (I usually look for a natural variety without sugar)

- tortilla wraps

- extra virgin olive oil, vinegar, lemon juice, and lime juice

Deli Section

- rotisserie chicken (I buy several when they are on sale. I immediately debone them and store half of each chicken in separate freezer bags for later meals.

- smoked salmon if you're making cucumber bites

- hummus

Dairy Section

- almond milk

- Greek yogurt

Freezer Section

- frozen corn

Chapter Summary

I hope you're listening to Coach John and revising your grocery habits. Once you begin clean eating, having tapas for supper, cutting back on red meat and sugar, you'll never look back.

- Spend your money on foods your grandma would recognize.

- Buy fresh, eat fresh.

- Get lots of whatever is on sale if you can freeze it or use it later.

- Eat lighter meals.

In the next chapter, you will learn a whole lot of new entree recipes for those dinner meals. Look for things your family will learn to love and get used to a couple of stunning recipes for company.

CHAPTER EIGHT

A WEEK OF SUPER BRAIN FOOD RECIPES

You may find this the most valuable chapter in the book. These recipes are your lifeline to a fully functioning mind, a brain working on all four cylinders. I'm excited for you!

Breakfast Recipes for a week of super brain functioning:

Sunday Morning Breakfast Casserole (serves 6)

Ingredients:

- 2 tablespoons fat of choice (extra virgin olive oil or ghee) melted

- 1 large sweet potato or yam, diced

- ½ teaspoon of fine sea salt

- 1 pepper, diced

- ½ yellow onion, diced

- 2 cups chopped spinach

- 10 eggs, whisked

- ½ teaspoon garlic powder

- ½ teaspoon salt

Directions:

1. Preheat your oven to 400°. Grease a 9x12 baking dish with sprayed olive oil.

2. Toss the diced sweet potatoes in olive oil and sprinkle with salt.

3. Place the sweet potatoes on a baking sheet and bake for 20-25 minutes, until soft.

4. While the sweet potatoes are baking, place a large sauté pan over medium heat. Add the onion and pepper. Cook until the onions are translucent and the peppers are soft.

5. Place your vegetable mix in the bottom of your baking dish. Add the sweet potatoes and spinach. Then add the eggs along with the garlic powder and second salt. Mix until well combined.

6. Place in the oven and bake for 25-30 minutes, until eggs are set in the middle.

Ezekiel French Toast (serves 1 or 2)

Ingredients:

- 2 slices of Ezekiel bread

- 2 eggs

- 2 tablespoons almond milk

- 1 tablespoon cinnamon

- 1 teaspoon raw honey (optional)

- 1 teaspoon coconut oil

- toppings of choice (I recommend pure maple syrup, and sliced strawberries, and bananas)

Instructions:

1. Heat a non-stick pan over a low to medium heat. Grease the pan with coconut oil.

2. Whisk the eggs, milk, cinnamon, and honey in a medium bowl. Transfer the egg mixture to a pie dish or low-set bowl.

3. Dunk the Ezekiel bread in the egg mixture for 15 seconds on each side.

4. Cook the Ezekiel bread for 2-3 minutes on each side, until golden brown.

5. Serve warm with toppings of choice.

Omelet Olé (serves 2)

Ingredients:

- extra virgin olive oil

- 4 eggs

- 1 tablespoon almond milk

- diced veggies of choice (peppers, onion, leftover sliced baked potato, etc.)

- 2 ounces crumbled fresh goat cheese (or grated cheese of choice)

- 2 cups baby spinach leaves

- diced cilantro

- sliced avocado

- ¼ cup Salsa Addiction

Instructions:

1. Drizzle extra virgin olive oil into a medium sauté pan on medium heat, add veggies and cook until soft.

2. Meanwhile, beat the eggs and milk in a small bowl.

3. Add the beaten eggs to the pan, then stir once, leave the vegetables mixed into the eggs. Reduce the heat to low for three minutes. Lift the edges of the egg mixture as it cooks and tilt the pan, letting the uncooked eggs fill the bottom. When it is slightly firm, add the goat cheese and fold the omelet onto its side. Cover the pan with foil and leave it on low heat for another few minutes until the eggs are cooked through. Turn the stove off and leave the pan covered, letting the residual heat "bake" it until the center is fully cooked.

4. Serve with avocado slices and salsa. You won't even miss the hash browns and toast!

Egg in a Basket (serves 2)
Ingredients:

- 2 eggs

- 1 tablespoon extra virgin olive oil

- 1 avocado halved

- salt and pepper

- Salsa Addiction

Directions:

1. Drizzle the olive oil in your sauté pan over medium heat.

2. When it is warm, crack your eggs into the pan, frying them as you prefer.

3. Slide each egg into half an avocado.

4. Top with salsa. Yum!

Busy Morning Oatmeal Buttermilk Pancakes (serves 4)

Ingredients:

- ½ cup water

- ½ cup instant dry milk

- 1 tablespoon honey

- 2 cups buttermilk

- 1 ½ cups rolled oats

- 1 cup whole wheat flour

- 1 teaspoon baking soda

- 1 to 2 beaten eggs

- 1 tablespoon coconut oil

- Fresh fruits and honey for toppings or Luscious Berry Syrup

Directions:

1. Mix the water, milk, and honey. Stir in the buttermilk. Add the rolled oats. Let the mixture refrigerate overnight to soften the oats.

2. Beat in the remaining ingredients.

3. Fry the pancakes on a hot griddle coated with melted coconut oil. Keep your heat low. When the pancakes are covered with bubbles, flip them and let them cook through.

4. Serve with toppings.

5. Luscious Berry Syrup: Puree a defrosted 16 ounce bag of frozen berries in your blender. Add 1 teaspoon cornstarch and boil over medium heat, stirring frequently. Cook until the mixture thickens. Serve warm over pancakes.

Granola (makes 12+ cups)
Ingredients:

- 7 cups rolled oats

- 1 cup wheat germ

- 1 cup bran flakes

- 1 ¼ cup sesame seeds

- ½ cup sunflower seeds

- ½ cup whole millet

- 2 tablespoons brewer's yeast

- 2 cups shredded coconut

- 2 cups pumpkin seeds

- 2 cups sliced almonds

- 1 cup chopped walnuts

- 3 cups dried fruits

- 1 cup honey

- 1 teaspoon vanilla

- ½ cup coconut oil

Instructions:

1. Heat your oven to 400°.

2. Put the oats in a baking pan or Dutch oven, and let them toast, shaking frequently.

3. Add the rest of the dry ingredients. Toast for another 5 minutes.

4. Add the coconut oil and honey and vanilla. Stir well. Toast 5 minutes more.

5. Store in an airtight container

Sunny Morning Wrap (serves 4)

Ingredients:

- 4 eggs

- ¼ teaspoon pepper, sprinkle of salt

- 1 cup of leftover rice

- 1 red pepper, diced

- coconut oil

- 4 six inch tortillas

- 4 ounces grated smoked cheese

- Salsa Addiction

Instructions:

1. Preheat the oven to 350°.

2. Drizzle coconut oil in a pan over medium heat. Cook the pepper until soft.

3. Reheat the rice in a microwave.

4. Whisk the eggs with salt and pepper.

5. Add the eggs to the vegetable mix, and cook, stirring to scramble the eggs.

6. Wrap the tortillas in foil and warm them in the oven for a few minutes.

7. To assemble, layer the egg and vegetable mix with rice, grated cheese, and salsa in the middle of a tortilla. Fold the left third to the center. Roll the bottom edge to the top.

8. Serve immediately, topping with more salsa. You can store them in an airtight container and reheat one or two wraps at a time in a microwave oven for 1 to 2 minutes.

Breakfast Rice Pudding (sort of) (serves 4)

Ingredients:

- Equal amounts brown rice and liquid in an instant pot. I use half water, half almond milk.

- Dried fruit.

- Cook on the rice setting.

- Serve with blueberries and almond milk.

Lunch Recipes

Warming Carrot, Ginger and Tumeric Soup (Serves 2)

Ingredients:

- 3 carrots, sliced

- 1 white onion, diced

- 3 cloves garlic, minced

- 1 inch piece of grated fresh ginger

- 2 inch piece of grated fresh turmeric

- 4 cups vegetable stock

- 1 tablespoon lemon juice

- Canned coconut milk (for topping)

- Sesame seeds (for topping)

Instructions:

1. Dice the onion and carrot into small chunks. (There is no need to be precise, as everything will be blended at the end.) Grate the ginger and turmeric finely.

2. Heat a small amount of extra virgin olive oil in the bottom of a large stock pot and saute the onion for 3 minutes until translucent. Add the garlic, turmeric and ginger. Sauté another minute.

3. Add the diced carrot and sauté another two or three minutes.

4. Add the vegetable stock and simmer for 20 to 25 minutes, until the carrots are cooked through and soft.

5. Transfer the soup into a standing blender and give it a spin to process the ingredients smoothly.

6. Stir in the lemon juice.

7. Serve with a swirl of coconut milk and top with some sesame seeds.

Good Medicine Chicken Vegetable Soup (serves 12-15)

Ingredients:

- A 3 or 4 pound chicken (stewing, broiler-fryer, thighs, drumsticks, breasts, etc. to equal poundage)

- 6 - 8 cups water

- 1 medium onion, diced

- 4 cloves garlic, minced

- 3-4 carrots, sliced

- 4 stalks celery with leaves, sliced

- 1 cup brown rice

- 16 oz frozen corn or 15 oz canned whole corn, drained

- 16 oz frozen green beans or 15 oz canned green beans, drained

- 4 large diced potatoes

- 1 pound of pasta (unless rice is used). Rotini, corkscrew, bowtie, ribbons, wagon wheel, orzo, any flavor

- ½ cup fresh flat-leaf parsley, chopped or ¼ cup dried parsley

- ½ fresh thyme, chopped or ¼ cup dried thyme

- 1 cup green or red cabbage, sliced

Instructions:

1. Prepare chicken and stock: Place chicken in a large Dutch oven and add enough water to cover. Leave the lid ajar for steam to escape, bring to boiling. Simmer until the chicken is tender, about one hour. Remove the chicken, strain the broth. When the chicken is cool enough to handle, remove meat from the bone. Discard the skin and bones. Use as directed below or save for another day.

2. Sauté the onion and garlic in a small drizzle of extra virgin olive oil. Add to the broth.

3. Add the carrots, celery, rice, frozen vegetables to the broth. Simmer until the carrots are soft.

4. Add the potatoes and pasta.

5. Add herbs, cabbage, and cook just until the cabbage is starting to soften, but still a tad crispy.

Taco Verdes (serves 2)
Ingredients:

- 4 tortillas

- 8 ounces tofu

- 1 ripe avocado

- 2 tablespoons lemon juice

- ¼ cup coconut oil

- 1 teaspoon fresh dill, minced

- ½ teaspoon salt

- ¼ cup water

- 1 can drained black beans

- 1 small onion, diced

- 2 cups lettuce and sprouts

- Salsa Addiction

Instructions:

1. In a blender; pureé tofu, avocado, lemon juice, oil, seasonings, and water.

2. Sauteé the onion until translucent. Add the black beans and heat through.

3. Make tacos with the black beans, blended mix, veggies and salsa in each tortilla.

Extreme Salad Bowl (serves 8)

Ingredients:

- Red lettuce, 1 head

- Romaine lettuce, 1 head

- Fresh spinach, 1 bag baby leaves

- 1 teaspoon lemon pepper

- 1 can drained garbanzo beans

- 1 can drained black beans

- 1 head broccoli

- 1 head cauliflower

- 2 peppers, one green and one red, cut into thin strips.

- ½ cup sliced almonds

- ½ cup dried cranberries

- 1 cup blueberries

- ¼ cup sunflower seeds

- ¼ cup pumpkin seeds

- ½ cup plain Greek yogurt

- 2 tablespoons dill, minced

Instructions:

1. Break the greens into bite-sized pieces

2. Generously sprinkle the greens with lemon pepper, toss.

3. Add the drained beans.

4. Cut broccoli and cauliflower florets and add.

5. Add the pepper strips.

6. Add all the nuts and seeds and fruits.

7. Mix the dressing of yogurt and dill, add, and toss well.

Egg Salad in a Bowl (serves 4)

Ingredients:

- 6 hard boiled, peeled eggs

- Mayonnaise and mustard

- Salt and pepper

- Two large tomatoes

Instructions:

1. Dice the hard boiled eggs.

2. Add mayonnaise and mustard and stir to moisten and hold the eggs together.

3. Season with salt and pepper.

4. Halve the tomatoes and dig out the pulp.

5. Serve with the egg salad in the hollowed tomatoes.

Tabouleh in a Jar (serves 2)

Ingredients:

- 2 cups water

- 2 bouillon cubes

- 2 cups bulgur wheat or cracked wheat

- 1 cup chopped fresh flat-leaf parsley

- ½ cup chopped onions

- 2 fresh tomatoes, chopped

- 2 T minced fresh mint

- ¾ cup lemon juice (approximately juice of 4 lemons)

- ½ cup extra virgin olive oil

- Surprise additions: broccoli florets, chopped zucchini, cauliflower florets

Instructions:

1. Soak the water, bouillon, and wheat in warm water for at least an hour, or until the liquid is absorbed.

2. Add to the wheat the parsley, onions, tomatoes, lemon juice and oil.

3. Add favorite extras.

4. Toss it all together lightly and parcel it into pint canning jars. Stash them in the fridge to grab on the way out the door to work in the morning.

Sunday Dinner and Night Time Suppers

Chicken Piccata

Ingredients:

- 2 boneless chicken breasts butterflied and patted dry

- ⅓ cup almond flour

- 5 tablespoons extra virgin olive oil

- 6 tablespoons coconut oil

- ⅓ cup fresh lemon juice (two to three lemons)

- ¼ cup capers

- ⅓ cup fresh flat-leaf parsley chopped

- salt and pepper to taste

- 5 ounces baby portabella mushrooms, sliced

- 2 cups chicken broth

- 2 cups brown rice

Instructions:

1. Place the chicken broth and brown rice with appropriate seasonings in your instant pot. Set for rice and ignore it.

2. Season the chicken with salt and pepper. Pour almond flour in a bowl and dredge both sides, shaking off the excess.

3. In a large skillet over medium-high heat, melt 2 tablespoons of coconut oil with 3 tablespoons of olive oil. When it starts to sizzle, add 2 pieces of chicken and cook for three minutes, or until browned. Flip and cook the other side. Remove and transfer to a plate. If you are cooking for more people, replenish the coconut and olive oil in the pan and continue to cook more chicken.

4. With one tablespoon coconut oil, sauté the mushrooms. Remove with the chicken.

5. Return the pan to the stovetop and add the lemon juice, stock, and capers. Bring to a boil, scraping up the brown bits from the pan for extra flavor. Taste to check the seasoning, then return the chicken and mushrooms to the pan for five minutes.

6. Plate the chicken over the bed of rice. Add remaining coconut oil to the sauce and whisk it thoroughly. Pour the sauce over the chicken and garnish with parsley.

Baked Chicken and Orzo (serves 2)

Ingredients:

- 1 cup orzo

- 1 cup chicken broth

- 2 four or five-ounce white fish fillets (cod, haddock or other fresh fish from your local supermarket)

- 2 cloves of garlic, crushed

- 1 tablespoon extra virgin olive oil

- 1 pint of cherry or grape tomatoes, halved

- 1 tablespoon white wine

- ¼ cup of black or kalamata olives, pitted

- handful of fresh basil, finely chopped

Instructions:

1. Put the orzo and broth into your instant pot and set to rice. Ignore it.

2. Pour the olive oil into a large oven-safe skillet set over medium heat. When shimmering, add the garlic. Cook, stirring it often. Burnt garlic turns bitter. It should be fragrant but not brown. One to two minutes.

3. Add the tomatoes. Stir in the white wine. Remove from heat.

4. Season the fish fillets. Place them into the pan so they touch the bottom of the pan. Top the two fillets with olives and basil leaves. Spoon some of the tomatoes and pan juice over the tops of the filets.

5. Transfer the skillet to the oven and bake until the fish is done, ten to fifteen minutes.

6. Serve with orzo and sauteéd zucchini or summer squash.

Coconut Curry Roasted Sweet Potatoes (serves 2)

Ingredients:

- 2 large sweet potatoes, rinsed, scrubbed and dried. Cut off any bruised spots. Cut into 2-inch chunks

- 2 tablespoons coconut oil, melted

- 1 tablespoon curry powder

- 1 teaspoon Himalayan sea salt to taste

Instructions:

1. Preheat the oven to 415°.

2. In a large mixing bowl, toss the sweet potato cubes with the melted coconut oil, curry powder and sea salt until the potatoes are thoroughly coated with both the oil and the spices.

3. Spread the seasoned potatoes in a large baking dish, and place them on the middle rack of the oven.

4. Set the timer for forty-five minutes. Flip the potatoes every fifteen minutes to avoid burning.

Seafood Chowder (serves 4)

Ingredients:

Fish broth:

- 3 to 4 pounds of fish heads. Be sure the skin, bones, fins, and tails are removed.

- Salt

- 2 tablespoons coconut oil

- 1 chopped onion

- 2 chopped carrots

- 2 stalks of chopped celery, including leaves

- 1 cup white wine

- 1 handful of dried mushrooms, preferably matsutake

- 2 bay leaves

Chowder:

- 1 tablespoon coconut oil

- 1 cup chopped yellow or white onion

- 2 celery stalks chopped. Use the leaves.

- 1 ½ pounds peeled and diced potatoes

- 5 to 6 cups fish broth or 4 cups chicken broth plus one to two cups water

- 1 to 2 pounds of fish cut into chunks

- 1 cup of corn, fresh or thawed

- ⅔ cup of cream

- black pepper to taste

- 2 tablespoons chopped fresh dill or chives for garnish

Instructions:

1. To make the broth, bring a large pot of water to a boil and salt it well. Add the fish heads. When the water returns to a boil, cook 1 minute. Remove bits of fish and save them, but discard the water. Blanching this way will give you a cleaner-tasting broth when you are done.

2. Wipe out the pot. Add the oil and turn the heat to medium-high. When the oil is hot, add the onion, carrot, and celery, stirring often. The onion should be cooked in four to five minutes. Add the white wine to deglaze the pan. Use a wooden spoon to scrape up any browned bits from the bottom. Add the bay leaves and dried mushrooms. Let the wine boil for a minute or two, then add the blanched fish. Cover with enough cool water to cover everything by about ½ inch. Bring to a very gentle simmer (barely bubbling) and cook for forty-five minutes.

3. Get a large bowl for the broth and set a strainer over it. Line the strainer with a plain paper towel or cheesecloth. Turn off the heat under the broth and ladle it through the strainer and into the bowl. Don't bother trying to get the last bits of broth from the pan, because it will be full of debris. Discard the contents of the pan and the strainer, but retain the broth.

4. To make the chowder, melt the coconut oil over medium heat. Add the onion and celery and sauté until soft. Add the potatoes and fish or chicken broth and bring to a simmer. Add salt to taste. Cook until the potatoes are tender, about fifteen to twenty minutes

5. Add the corn and chunks of fish. Cook gently until the fish is just cooked through, about five minutes. Turn off the heat and stir in the herbs, heavy cream and black pepper.

Pesto Pasta (serves 5-6)

Ingredients:

- one 16-oz package pasta of choice (rotini, corkscrew, bowtie, ribbons, etc. Any flavor)
- 2 cups fresh basil leaves
- 1 cup pine nuts
- 1 clove minced garlic
- ½ Parmesan cheese
- 1 tablespoon grated cheese
- ½ almond milk
- 8 oz unflavored Greek yogurt
- ½ teaspoon salt
- pinch cayenne pepper

Instructions:

1. Cook pasta following the package instructions.

2. In a blender or food processor, blend the basil leaves, pine nuts, garlic, cheese, lemon juice, and almond milk until nicely chopped. Add yogurt, salt, and pepper and process the pesto until smooth, stopping to scrape the sides as necessary.

3. Drain the pasta well. Return it to the same pan. Add the pesto and mix well to coat evenly. Transfer to a serving dish and garnish with basil leaves if desired.

Spanish Bulgur Wheat (serves 2)

Ingredients:

- two tablespoons coconut oil

- 1 clove minced garlic

- ½ cup chopped green onions

- ½ green pepper, diced

- 1 ¼ cups bulgur wheat

- 1 cup cooked kidney or pinto beans

- 1 teaspoon paprika

- salt to taste

- ¼ teaspoon black pepper

- eight to ten tomatoes

Instructions:

1. Heat the oil in a skillet and sauté the garlic, green onions, green pepper, and bulgur until the bulgur is coated with oil and the onions are translucent.

2. Add the beans, paprika, and seasonings.

3. Blanch the tomatoes to remove the skins, chop and add.

4. Cover and bring to a boil, then reduce the heat and simmer until the liquid is absorbed and the bulgur is tender, about fifteen minutes. Add chicken broth or water if more liquid is needed.

Lasagne Swirls (serves 4-6)

Ingredients:

- eight lasagne noodles

- 2 pounds fresh spinach

- 2 tablespoons Parmesan cheese

- 1 cup ricotta cheese

- ¼ teaspoon nutmeg

- 2 tablespoons coconut oil

- 2 cloves minced garlic

- ½ cup chopped onion

- 2 cups tomato sauce

- ½ teaspoon basil

- ½ teaspoon oregano

Instructions:

1. Cook and drain the noodles until al dente. Set aside. Preheat the oven to 350°.

2. Wash the spinach, put it in a pan with a tight-fitting lid, and wilt it about seven minutes over medium heat.

3. Drain the spinach and squeeze it in cheesecloth or paper towels to remove any excess moisture. Mix it with the cheeses, nutmeg. Season the mixture with salt and pepper.

4. Coat each noodle with the mixture and roll them up. Place in a shallow baking pan with the open side down.

5. Heat the coconut oil and sauté the garlic and onion until the onion is translucent. Add the tomato sauce and herbs. simmer, season to taste.

6. Pour the sauce over the noodles and bake for twenty minutes in the heated oven.

What about those times when a sugar craving just knocks your socks off? When you need to binge watch something and munching is in order? Well, I have a few healthy recipes for just those situations. You can only eat berries or dessert so many times before you just naturally rebel, and remember, I emphasized baby steps!

High Protein Chocolate Chip Cookies

Preheat the oven to 375°. I use parchment paper on the cookie sheets because I don't like to wash the pans, so if you're like me, line those baking sheets before you begin mixing. This isn't a purist version of cookies, it's the kind that allows you to fudge while still stocking up on protein.

Ingredients:

- 1 cup of butter (two sticks)

- ¾ cup of stevia or erythritol brown sugar (alright, use the regular if you must!)

- ¾ cup of stevia or erythritol (or white sugar if you're suffering)

- 2 eggs

- ⅓ cup powdered milk

- 1 teaspoon baking soda

- 2 cups whole wheat flour

- 1 teaspoon salt

- 1 package chocolate chips (I recommend the Lily sugar-free chips, but I've thrown up my hands, here.)

- ½ cup chopped nuts (unsalted peanuts or cashews or walnuts

- ½ cup of unsalted sunflower seeds or pumpkin seeds

Directions:

1. Cream the butter until it's soft.

2. Add the sugars and blend until it's well mixed.

3. Add the eggs.

4. I'm lazy and add all of my dry ingredients in a well on the side of the bowl at one time. Then I mix them in completely.

5. Add the chips, nuts, and seeds.

6. Drop onto the parchment-lined baking sheets in spoonfuls according to how big you want your want your cookies. Bake 8-10 minutes. If they spread out too much, you need more flour. If they are too poofy you added too much flour.

Wine

Remember I told you that a glass of wine is actually good for you? I grew up in a teetotal household and had to learn how to pair wines for satisfying results. Here are some tips you may find helpful:

- Your wine should be both more acidic and sweeter than your food.

- Your wine should be as intense as the food on your menu.

- A white wine pairs better with chicken and seafood.

Gourmands will describe twenty different flavors in food. I found that pretty amazing. These include the usual sweet and sour, and proceed into much more eclectic sensations. To pair wine, you just need to know three things. How sweet is the wine? How bitter is the wine? How acidic is the wine?

I go by two basic principles: Do I like it? Is it for dinner or dessert? See how easy that was? For dinner wines, I get a basic white or red (if I'm serving beef). For dessert, I like a Moscato or sparkling wine. One glass a day. Remember wine is high in calories, so it's just like dark chocolate. One serving. Be honest and don't fudge on this!

Chapter Summary

By now you should be feeling comfortable with the recipes that nourish your brain. You will need to compile your own grocery list this time because I have to way of knowing how soon and how fast you'll dive into this world of brain-boosting menus. Are you adding your checkmarks to your calendar? If you are still with me, you are within a couple of months of living with a super-charged brain. I'm proud of you!

- What you've noticed in this chapter is how easy it is to find and fix brain foods.

- Did you notice the lack of red meat? I specifically offered you recipes to complement the ones you already know.

- Remember to add these new dishes into your regimen slowly. You don't have to divorce yourself from a good steak. A cordial separation with visiting rights will do.

In the next chapter, you will learn how to detox your brain. That sounds scary, doesn't it? It's okay, I promise.

CHAPTER NINE

HOW TO DETOX TO IMPROVE BRAIN HEALTH

We hear a lot about detoxing, but let's be sure we're all on the same page here. Physiologically, it's a cellular function your body labors at incessantly. As your cells detoxify, they package the leftover debris in the form of food and secretions being excreted from the body. Obviously, the food exits via the alimentary tract. But you also excrete toxins via the respiratory tract, through sweat, and via the genitourinary tract. To accomplish this task, your liver, lungs, gallbladder, skin, kidneys and yes, your brain, all get involved.

Of all the organs in your body, your brain suffers the most when toxins circulate through your system. You hear about assaults like tobacco, medications, inflammatory foods, alcohol, drugs, heavy metals, microorganisms, chemicals, and environmental pollutants all the time, but the natural assumption is that they affect specific organs and the bloodstream. Few stop to consider what happens when they cross the blood-brain barrier and invade the inner sanctum of thought and function.

This happens as your natural defenses get overwhelmed. Unhealthy metabolites trigger mitochondrial dysfunction and rogue cells get reproduced. Metabolic deficiencies, immunotoxicity, and neuroinflammation (inflammation of the brain) begin to affect your system. As a result, your body's energy is diverted to hot spots, like the brain. The heart and muscles suffer, and you experience fatigue, mental fog, cognitive difficulties.

You're starting your program of clean eating, learning to follow the MIND protocols, but there are still toxins lurking in your brain, and you need to get rid of that nastiness as soon as possible. If you're ready to turn over a new leaf, let's detoxify!

I'm going to suggest you embark on a comprehensive elimination diet. For some of you, this will look different than for others. Some of you aren't diabetic, but you are sensitive to sugar. Some of you are sensitive to salt and bloat when you indulge in salty snacks. Some of you are thinking, *I don't have problems like that, I don't need this!* Here's the thing. You don't have problems like that *yet*. You still need to detoxify.

Begin by focusing on what you're eating. Eat as many colors as you can in an array of different fruits and vegetables. All these colors contain vitamins and nutrients essential to the process. Include ginger, turmeric, garlic, beets, broccoli seed sprouts, and herbs like thyme and rosemary in your diet each day. Eat dark leafy vegetables and cruciferous vegetables like cabbage. Eat nuts, legumes and fatty foods like avocados and bananas. Does this sound familiar? You're already on the right track, aren't you?

Add to it interval eating. It's called **intermittent fasting**. Allow your body to take a break from constantly digesting, letting your divert energy from the GI tract to the organs your body uses for detoxification. Consult your doctor, but realize you don't have to go overboard. A simple intermittent fasting pattern allows your body to focus its energy on those organs that detoxify rather than the alimentary tract eating yet another meal.

This may be a new concept for you, but in reality, its roots lie in ancient times. Many religions fast to draw closer to the Almighty, and there are those who recommend "fasting" as a form of dieting, but it's time to look at what fasting is and is not. Fasting is not starving yourself to lose weight. It is the voluntary control of your food intake apart from the societal norms of three meals a day. Look at the process of your normal day.

You rise and "break the fast" of a night's rest. When you eat, your body spikes insulin to cover the expected influx of nutrients. Of course, you're probably eating more than you need for the moment, so your body processes the extra into glycogen (stored sugar deposited in the liver). As the day progresses the storage space for all that glycogen gets overloaded and your body begins to transfer that glycogen into fat (also stored in the liver, though I find a lot around my waistline). In the course of all these meals, your body doesn't have time to deal with increasing levels of toxins and it's like an accident looking for a place to happen.

When you fast, the opposite takes place. Your body changes its reservoir of fat into glycogen. That glycogen is then metabolized into glucose. Your body "feasts" on the fat of the land. See a doctor and be safe. Begin with a simple goal in mind. Fast one meal, and see how your body reacts to the experiment. Then expand your efforts. Design a plan, like twice a week eating for eight hours and fasting for sixteen. Some fast twenty-fours twice a week.

Remember that the goal is detoxification. You don't need to go overboard. Just give your body a rest from its normal job of processing too much food, and it will begin its clean up and internal regimen. These are the known physiological benefits of intermittent fasting:

- reduction of oxidative stress (that overload of too many free radicals we talked about)

- detoxification of your system

- resetting your insulin levels

- putting your body into ketosis (burning fat for sugar to provide energy)

- anti-aging benefits

- higher levels of human growth hormone

- reducing blood levels of triglycerides

During your detox, try to minimize toxins and food contaminants. Look for organic produce to minimize exposure to pesticides and farm chemical residues. Use eco-friendly cosmetics, personal care products, and cleaning agents. Paying attention to what you eat and use opens

114

your eyes to how widespread the level of contamination is in our environment.

At the same time, increase your level of exercise. Run, walk, enroll in a yoga class, dance or bike. Just get your body moving and start sweating. That's right. Eliminate those toxins!

Don't forget to watch your water intake. Fill up your water bottle several times a day. Your body needs to flush out the toxins, but how can it if it's dehydrated? We're talking about water here, not counting that guilty indulgence of soda at lunch or your morning coffee. Drink water to detoxify.

Chapter Summary

Everyone wants to detox these days, but they usually want to do it for all the wrong reasons. The most important organ in your body is your brain. Let's expunge those pesky toxins to remain vital and alert.

- Detoxing your brain isn't difficult. Watch what you eat. Drink lots of water. Exercise.

- Intermittent fasting is great for detoxing, and a healthy lifestyle to adopt.

- We're talking about a way of living, not a one-time fix.

In the next chapter, you will learn how to be healthy, stay healthy. It's all about your immune system and revving it up to full potential.

CHAPTER TEN

BOOST YOUR IMMUNE SYSTEM

We talk about our immune systems in terms of disease prevention, and rightfully so. Remember that event you went to the other night? The one where that poor soul hacked halfway through the event? Walking germs spread disease, true, but do you have to be the next victim?

When we talk about your ability to ward off disease, we talk about several basic factors. How virulent is the organism causing disease? Is this a bug that's been running its course over several days, or is this some superbug causing a worldwide plague? That answer depends a lot on you. How well rested are you? How strong is your immune system? Your body can fight off most infections if it is armed to the teeth with the right systemic warriors and if you are functioning at peak performance. Obviously, all of this affects your ability to think, process information, work at top efficiency. Let's look at what comprises your **immune system** and how you can improve it.

You may be surprised to learn that a small war has been going on for all of your life in the backstreets of your body. Your skin is your first line of defense. The bronchi in your lungs try to breathe out gaseous toxins, and your stomach acid labors to neutralize those ingested toxins. Some toxins leak through these defense mechanisms. Once a pathogen enters your system, the war is on.

Your lymph system, spleen, tonsils, and thymus are major players in producing agents to fight invading pathogens. You may be surprised to learn that your bowel plays an important part in this process as well. I know, right? Over and over again, you're learning that what you eat and how it is digested is a much bigger deal than you ever imagined. Listen to Coach Josh once again. The complex network of cells and systems keeping you healthy rely heavily on your gut. They rely on a healthy gut.

As many as seventy percent of your immune cells reside along the pathways of your intestinal tract. The lining of your intestines secrete antibodies that identify and destroy harmful bacteria. Your alimentary tract also synthesizes vitamins and compounds that either work for you or against you. When the body wages war upon itself, we call it an autoimmune disease. These take the form of chronic and often debilitating diseases that may plague you your entire life. If you know anyone with lupus, rheumatoid arthritis, fibromyalgia, you already know you want to avoid contracting these ailments.

Let's reinforce what we've already learned:

- for optimal gut health, you need probiotics

- processed foods have their innate goodness processed right out of them

- cooking from scratch with real ingredients helps

- clean eating means you're ingesting real food

- organic meats and produce mean you're cutting out the pesticides you don't want to eat

Talk with your doctor or a holistic health provider about potential food sensitivities. You may want to remove gluten, dairy, or soy from your diet. Stool tests can assess gut bacterial levels and identify imbalances. The foods you eat and the way your body handles them matter, and it's your job to become the detective ferreting out information for your optimal health and brain function.

Another area to look into is your vitamin levels. What is circulating through your bloodstream? What basic ingredients does your brain have to work with in getting you through the day? Vitamin D is probably the single most important vitamin when we talk about your immune system. Many folks who are diagnosed with chronic ailments, like those autoimmune diseases, are walking around with low levels of vitamin D. Many doctors and holistic therapists recommend supplementation of 2,000 to 5,000 IU of vitamin D daily. Ask your doctor to check your level to determine the amount you need.

Another vitamin affecting your immune system is vitamin C. People under increased physical and especially emotional stress, find themselves at risk of the common cold. Remember we talked about the virility or strength of an organism in relation to how prepared you are to fight it off? When your body is stressed, it's not able to fight as well. Increase your levels of vitamin C to decrease your incidences of the common cold. Healthcare providers suggest taking supplements of

1,000 mg to 5,000 mg daily. If you're not eating your vitamin C, you may need supplementation.

Your immune system loves a balanced diet of whole, unprocessed foods with plenty of antioxidants. Does that sound familiar? What you're learning is the importance of the food you eat and how it affects not just your present health, but how you'll feel tomorrow, the next day, and ten years from now. Two superfoods affect your immune system. One is eating four or five servings a day of greens. Lettuce, mustard greens, collard greens, spinach, kale...you should know these by heart at this point! The other superfood may surprise you. Mushrooms. Did you know mushrooms are packed with vitamin D? Some studies suggest that various mushrooms offer much more. Maitake and reishi seem to boost white blood cell activity as well.

In addition, put more garlic into your menu. When it is crushed, garlic releases allicin, a compound that fights microbes causing infection.

Last but not least, you boost your immunity when you get adequate **sleep** at night. Healers recommend seven to eight hours a night, a luxury for most adults, but necessary nonetheless. Insufficient sleep lowers your ability to ward off disease. If you have trouble falling asleep or staying asleep throughout the night, speak with your physician. Chemical or hormonal imbalances may be the culprit. Try taking melatonin or valerian root prior to bedtime to improve the quality of your sleep.

Chapter Summary

To have a strong immune system, you need to protect and nourish your brain.

- Eat foods rich in Vitamins C and D.

- Eat a well-balanced diet with greens in every meal. Eat more fresh mushrooms.

- Sleep like your life depends on it. It does.

FINAL WORDS

Thank you for inviting me into your home, for taking the time to read and digest this material, for allowing me to be your motivational coach. If you have kept your intake records and been adjusting your eating habits, you are noticing a visible difference in both how you look and how you feel. If you've been slow to get on board, it's not too late. That's the beauty of having this book. You can jump back on the wagon when you feel the effects of too much indulging and recalibrate your system.

As your coach, I've tried to identify the issues underlying why you bought this book. I've tried to provide you a framework for understanding why you need to make a change, and I've offered you recipes to help you make those changes. Coaching is much more than that, however. As your coach, it's important that I've motivated you to see yourself for both where you are and where you want to be.

Take a moment, and list what you see in yourself right now. List the good habits, the indulgences, evidence of too much binging and not enough exercise.

Now list where you want to be. How would you change yourself if you could? If time and money were not an obstacle? List those changes, no matter how unattainable you deem them to be.

That space between the two lists is where motivation comes into play. To continue to make changes and become more healthy, you must remain motivated. Here are ways to pay yourself the richest of dividends: a newer, healthier you.

- Find an accountability partner and make a pact, set a goal.

- Continue to track your progress.

- Establish a notebook, or filing system, for healthy recipes

- Develop a meal plan your family will follow.

- Put together a master grocery list for weekly shopping.

- Keep taking baby steps. Don't make it too hard, and don't settle at what feels comfortable.

- Find the kind of exercise you enjoy and will do on a regular basis.

- Get a water bottle you like and keep it filled.

- Learn to cook from scratch.

You've read the book once and reached the very end. Now, go back and dog-ear the pages that were most helpful. Highlight those concepts you want to learn more about. Read the book again, more slowly, taking notes. This is where you find the gold. I know a few of you were speed readers. You scanned each chapter. You turned up your nose at some of the recipes. You shrugged and thought, huh! Now you're reading the Final Words to see if you really want to dive into the process of changing yourself. Let me promise you this: If you do, you will look back in three months, and be amazed at the change it has made in your life, your job, your relationships.

Your health is the one thing you may own without the intervening control of others. You can choose what to eat. You can choose to put down that soda and get a glass of cool, refreshing water. You can choose to eat less steak or fewer hamburgers, and eat more fish. You can choose to eat your greens. You can choose to walk more. No government, no boss, no friend is stopping you. It's all you. Ask yourself what your health is worth. These are not changes that will break the bank...but a major disease will. Try paying for a heart attack or dialysis. The time to make those changes is before it's too late to keep yourself healthy.

I know you want to make these changes because you picked up the book and came this far. Now go all the way. Go back and pick up those things that made you turn up your nose and find a way to work through them. Sometimes it takes a tragedy to make us willing to change, and I pray that's not true for you. Sometimes it's just a matter of picking yourself up by the collar and shaking yourself into caring and doing what needs to be done. Since I don't live near you, and we can't meet in weekly sessions, my pages must do the work for me. So go back. Reread the book. Do your homework. Control your destiny.

Learn as much as you can. I've given you a full list of resources, and you will learn a lot by reading other sources you find. This reading reinforces what you've learned and offers compounding interest in the object of increasing your motivation to become healthy, eat better, exercise more. In addition to reading more, follow good counsel. The world is full of peddlers selling easy cures to anything and everything that ails you.

Your health is too precious to try to self-medicate or to follow the wrong advice. Learn as much as you can, and get more than one opinion before making sweeping changes. Look critically at fad diets. Learn to recognize the credentials of the healthcare providers you trust, and look at their patients. Get recommendations. My biggest concern as your coach is that you may learn just enough to be a danger to yourself or become prey to someone who uses the right verbiage but who lacks the expertise to care for you. It's a dangerous world out there, my friends. Be smart, be vigilant.

Remember that good health comes from clean eating and lots of colors. I am not recommending pills or supplements or powders. I am not selling products of any kind. Instead, I want to sell you on health. Optimal health. Radiant health. Let me save you a fortune and a lot of time. Look at food as your friend, and let its colors heal you. Look at water as the source of life. Drink it. Look at exercise as the dance of life. Put some into your daily routine. This is Coach John signing off. Until we meet again, be happy. Be well. Be good to yourself.

GLOSSARY

Antioxidants--These are chemicals derived from the food we eat, and their main job lies in balancing the oxidants in your bloodstream. Let me break this down: Your body is a complex machine with all kinds of checks and balances, moves and counter moves. Oxidants are the leftover sludge when your body creates new chemicals metabolized from the food you eat.

The antioxidants are warrior compounds your body synthesizes to keep that nasty oxidation in check. One is glutathione, made from three amino acids: glutamine, glycine, and cysteine. Millions upon millions of chemical reactions are taking place in your body every single day. In the process, some compounds become unstable, with a free, or extra electron. (Think back to your ancient class on organic chemistry with the descriptions of protons and electrons in each element.) That tiny free electron is known as a *free radical*.

Your body produces some of these free radicals just in everyday living. It is exposed to some in smoking. radiation, and other pollutants. It acquires some as the result of stress and alcohol consumption. When the balance of antioxidants and free radicals gets out of whack, oxidative stress results. The stress weakens cell membranes. It damages connective tissue and collagen (think your knees!). It is a precursor to cancer and cardiovascular disease. It is a culprit in autoimmune diseases like arthritis and psoriasis. It affects diabetes. You cannot afford to ignore this all-important part of your dietary regimen.

The Autonomic Nervous System--It's often called the involuntary nervous system because it works while you sleep and without any self-direction. Losing control of muscles is the loss of personal autonomy, perhaps loss of a particular line of work, loss of cherished activities. Loss of your autonomic functions is disastrous. Your brain's function and heart's life depends on the body's ability to serve as the most efficient workhorse mankind has ever encountered.

It functions from your medulla, at the back of the brain, and is divided into two separate centers: the sympathetic and parasympathetic. These two control centers perform different functions, often turning on and turning off various switches. What does your dinner have to do with all of this? More than you think.

Let's look at just one of many examples. You get up in the morning and want to get that adrenaline flowing, signaling the sympathetic nervous system to get to work. It does its fight or flight thing all day long. It requires a neurotransmitter to pass along all these messages throughout your body. What happens when you want to go to bed at night? The parasympathetic works in direct opposition, using acetylcholine to signal for chemicals like serotonin to let you relax and go to sleep. Think of a little wheel in a hamster cage. The hamster runs and runs, spinning it in one direction. Then all of a sudden it stops, maybe nibbles a bite of food, and starts spinning the wheel in the opposite direction. Your brain is like that hamster's spinning wheel, and which way it spins depends on the neurotransmitters activating those nerve transmissions.

The neurotransmitters are chemicals your body makes and stores at nerve endings, ready to be activated upon command so different events may take place. They all use the same brain, the same nerves, the same junctions, but each neurotransmitter sets off a different kind of chemical reaction with a different kind of result. Your body synthesizes these neurotransmitters from the food you eat.

That sobering reality is often lost on us when we binge on chips and soda in front of the TV, isn't it? No wonder we function poorly! The supply chain for manufacturing these nerve conductions gets interrupted. Do that often and long enough, and biological mayhem takes place. If you want to avoid such a tragedy, eat your fruits, and vegetables, and whole grains. Those are the sources for the building blocks you need.

Clean Eating--There is a plethora of experts wanting to sell you on the concept of clean eating. Literally. *Enroll in my program (for a monthly fee), or buy my magazine.* You may want to do either or both, but realize what clean eating is. Then try it. Then see if you need to pay to be in a program, or want to purchase a magazine subscription.

Researchers describe clean eating in simple to understand terms:

- Eat real foods. We talked about that, right? Avoid processed foods, and eat things your grandmother would recognize.

- Eat to be healthy, not to feel pleasure.

- Eat more plants.

What is the opposite of clean eating? Food additives, for one thing. Avoid sugar substitutes like aspartame, a known neurotoxin. Monosodium glutamate (MSG) stimulates nerve cells, ultimately wearing them out. Some believe it blocks your sensation of feeling satisfied, leading you to eat more. Other people are just plain sensitive to it, experiencing headaches, nausea, flushing, or even palpitations upon ingesting it. Trans fats are additives to extend the shelf life of processed foods.

You can find them in the labels under monikers like lauric acid, myristic acid, variations of linoleic acid, and arachidonic acid. Food colorings are added to processed foods because their natural colorings have either been stripped away in processing or to entice the buyer into picking up an attractive package. Every colored additive is linked to research on various carcinomas or diseases. Sodium sulfite, sodium nitrates, and sodium nitrites are other preservatives to avoid. BHA and BHT are added to processed foods to prevent them from changing color and to keep them from becoming rancid. Sulfur dioxide is a preservative that destroys your body's vitamin E. Potassium bromate is added to bakery products.

Are you seeing the pattern here? When you look at labels and have trouble reading some of the words, put the food down. Those hard-to-read additives are the opposite of clean eating. Eat the food. Not the way manufacturers have processed the food.

Flavonoids--These powerful derivatives of the foods you eat interact with enzymes for peak performance. One study describes their ability to increase interactions with neuroproteins and facilitate vascular connections with increased blood supply. Many of the preliminary studies suggest a vital connection between your brain health and these basic building blocks.

In plants, they are a part of basic processes of using ultraviolet rays in photosynthesis and utilizing nitrogen in healthy plant life. The Linus Pauling Institute describe six different varieties of these micronutrients: anthocyanidins (berries, grapes and wine), flavan-3-oils (tea, cocoa, berries, grapes, and apples), flavanones (onions, broccoli, berries, apples, and teas), flavones (citrus fruits and juices), and isoflavones (soy and legumes). The most common of these are the flavonols. They benefit the plants, and when you eat them, they continue to benefit you as well.

When you eat these colorful fruits and vegetables, enjoy chocolate, drink wine or oolong tea, you ingest these compounds and they are metabolized or transformed into chemicals that signal your body to undertake anti-inflammatory, antidiabetic, and anticancer actions. The clinical trials are promising enough to suggest you take notice. At this point the evidence is sketchy, but researchers are hopeful they can prove their value in neuroprotective mechanisms. This would herald a change in the way we treat dementia by preventing it altogether. I am expecting evidence to prove this true and recommending we eat as if it will be true.

It will only make you healthier, and if it prevents Alzheimer's disease, what a great plus!

Immune system--Your immune system is a much larger part of your body than you may recognize. We talked about your skin being your first line of defense, but what you may not realize is that epithelial cells (like skin) are warriors that line every surface of your body exposed to the outside world. Your throat, intestines, blood vessels, and all your organs, have an epithelial lining. Look in an old biology book for a review: Some are flat (squamous epithelial cells lining blood vessels and lungs), cuboidal (in your kidneys and other glands), columnar (in your intestines, nose, and throat), and ciliated (lined with small hairs that push mucus around).

If your body isn't successful in warding off a microbe, it goes to war internally. If you review further, you'll remember a chapter about humoral immunity, which is where your body forms a second line of defense. The two most common are the blood-brain barrier and the blood-cerebrospinal fluid barrier. Each tries to filter out microbes before they can infect the brain or your nervous system, which controls the entire body.

If they get past the first line of defense, it's war. Your white blood cells only comprise about 1% of your blood, yet they work tirelessly. There are five types:

- monocytes--these break down the cell wall of bacteria

- leukocytes--these cells create antibodies to fight bacteria and viruses

- neutrophils--these cells hemolyze and digest bacteria

- eosinophils--attack cancer cells and allergens

- basophils--signal the release of histamine and other chemicals fighting allergic reactions

Once you're infected with a disease, your white blood cells and their support systems come into play. They produce interferon, which tries to disrupt viruses, and macrophages to carry away dead material. If the disease microbes enter your cells, phagocytosis (by way of leukocytes) begins, trying to surround the invading cells and overpower them. Granulocytes (neutrophils. eosinophils and basophils) attack the proteins of the bacteria and neutralize them.

When you get sick and visit your doctor, you may have blood drawn to analyze your white blood cells. A normal result is 5000-10,000 wbc. If a differential count is ordered, you'll see a lot of numbers that may seem meaningless to you at first glance. This chart shows what a healthy blood count would look like.

White Blood Cell by Type	Percentage in the Blood Count
neutrophil	55 to 73%
lymphocyte	20-40%
eosinophil	1-4%

monocyte	2-8%
basophil	0.5-1%

Determining which cells are present, if they are high or low, helps determine the kind of infection your body is fighting.

Seriously, this reads like an epic saga of good and evil, with heroic forces fighting against overwhelming odds at times, all in an effort to keep you alive. Everything you can do to boost your immune system provides these white blood cells with the energy and resources to wage that war. When you deprive them of what they need through a poor diet, through staying up late, etc., you leave yourself vulnerable to disease.

What happens when your immune systems run amok? If your body goes overboard and produces too many white blood cells, you are diagnosed with leukemia or lymphoma. Another problem occurs if your system produces too many cells and they never mature. That is a myeloproliferative disorder and is diagnosed upon finding an imbalance of cells. If your body goes overboard in waging war and begins to mistake your cells as the enemy, you develop an autoimmune disease like lupus, fibromyalgia, arthritis, psoriasis, etc. The body begins to attack itself.

All of this indicates the importance of keeping a healthy immune system in peak condition.

Intermittent fasting--Research is replete with the evidence: we eat too much too often. Giving your body a break from its incessant need to digest more and more food yields many benefits. The benefits revolve around four basic changes that occur while your body is resting:

- Insulin levels drop significantly, and as a result, you start burning fat.

- Your blood levels of growth hormone increase. A lot. That also facilitates burning fat while boosting muscle growth.

- Your body initiates important repair processes, like transporting waste to excretion depots.

- This is a big one. Your body engages several genes and molecules related to your immune system and longevity.

This all takes place when you participate in an intermittent fasting cycle. We're not talking about crash diets. It's more like scheduled retreats from food. Two or three days a week you adapt to a program of 8 hours of meals with 16 hours of no food or water. Some fast from food and water twenty-four hours twice a week. Talk to your doctor. Take a trial run. Figure out what works for you. These are some of the other benefits you'll enjoy.

1. Of course, you'll lose that stubborn belly fat. Expect a slimmer waistline.

2. Unless you're binge eating during your other hours, you'll also lose weight.

3. You'll lower your risk of Type 2 diabetes.

4. You'll decrease the inflammation and oxidative stress in your body.

5. There is no conclusive proof, but there is some promising evidence that fasting reduces the risk of cancer.

The benefits to your brain are what we are most concerned about here. Intermittent fasting increases levels of a brain hormone called *brain-derived neurotrophic factor (BDNF)*. Scientists believe a deficiency of this hormone is responsible for depression and other mental health issues. It is thought that fasting reduces the risk of a stroke, though that may be a result of healthier eating at the same time. Researchers think it may delay the onset of Alzheimer's disease, or at least reduce its severity. This lifestyle change improved Alzheimer's symptoms in nine out of ten patients.

One of the most common methods of intermittent fasting involves restricting meals to a short window of eight hours out of twenty-four. I find it easier to fast through my day of work. I'm able to accomplish more and my mind is sharper. I eat a meal in the evening and graze on nuts or dried fruit when I veg out to unwind.

The evidence is compelling, while not conclusive. It is compelling enough to make me change my patterns, and recommend it to my clients. Your heart will thank you. You will experience a decreased risk of cancer. Your body will have the energy to engage in gene repair. You'll probably live longer.

The Japanese Diet--Based on "washoku," traditional Japanese cuisine, those who adopt this diet eat smaller servings in dishes made with simple, fresh ingredients. Think about dining out at an oriental restaurant. No one gets a dinner plate the size of a wok. Rather, delicacies are served on dainty little dishes and tempt the palate without putting it to sleep with way too much heavy food. A great emphasis is put on making it pleasing to the eye, making part of the feast visual rather than palate sensitive.

The foods in the Japanese diet center around fish, various noodles, tofu, steamed rice, seaweed, and freshly cooked fruits, and vegetables. Some pickled or fermented ingredients balance the flavors and add probiotics to the mix. What you don't see is a lot of eggs, dairy or meat. Those occur in very small, complementary amounts. These meals are characterized by a fifth kind of taste bud sensation, a rich umami flavor, as it is called. Much of it centers around sushi rice, which is prepared with vinegar to make it sticky. That vinegar; does it make a difference?

According to research accepted by the World Health Organization, women eating this diet typically live to 87 years of age, and the men live to an average of 80 years. Studied subjects not only live longer, they exhibit less hypertension, less cardiac disease, fewer strokes, and enjoy better joint health. You don't have to eat raw fish to put some of their practices into effect. Eat smaller portions on tinier dishes. Use more vegetables and fruits. Eat less meat. Make your meals aesthetically pleasing. Live longer and better.

The Mediterranean Diet--Scientists noticed longevity and healthier lifestyles among those living along the Mediterranean Sea. It wasn't their doctors or their pharmacies. It was their dinner plates. It is regarded as heart-healthy. It includes a daily inclusion of vegetables, fruits, whole grains, and healthy fats. Each week there are fish, poultry, beans, and eggs. There are moderate dairy and less red meat. It includes sharing the meal with family or friends, enjoying a glass of red wine and lots of talks. It is plant-based, not meat-based.

This diet incorporates healthy fats as a mainstay, with fewer saturated and trans fats known to cause coronary disease. Olive oil is a monounsaturated fat lowering cholesterol and low-density lipoproteins (LDL) levels. Nuts and seeds, also prominent in their recipes, also contain monounsaturated fats. So are fatty fish such as mackerel, herring, sardines, albacore tuna, salmon. All are rich in omega-3 fatty acids, which are known to reduce inflammation. Omega-3 fatty acids provide other benefits, like reducing the risk of heart failure and stroke.

Typical health benefits are lower cardiovascular disease, less diabetes, lower blood pressure, less dementia, and a longer lifespan. The better health of people on this diet was first noted back in the 1950s and study after study since then has confirmed it. By contrast, the typical American diet of meat and potatoes, skip the green, please, is a killer.

Omega-3 Fatty Acids--Basically, there are two essential fatty acids: Alpha-linolenic acid (one of many omega-3 fatty acids) and linoleic acid (an omega-6 fatty acid). Theoretically, your body can manufacture everything you need from just these two substances.

Notice I said, "theoretically." The truth is, sometimes it doesn't and that's where diet comes into play. The good fat is essential. Two are critical: EPA (eicosapentaenoic acid) and DHA (docosahexaenoic acid). Don't ask me who named them. Why would anyone give something essential such a jawbreaker of a name? They are found in certain fish. ALA (alpha-linolenic acid) is found in plant sources like nuts and seeds.

The list of maladies affected by not having enough omega-3 fatty acids reads like a program at a conference of the AMA. Rheumatoid arthritis, depression, Alzheimer's disease, fetal development, ADHD, and asthma all point to deficient omega-3s as co-conspirators in disease processes. The old quack doctors selling serum that would cure everything from snake bite to palsy were not so far off base as once thought. It is true that some very basic building blocks form the basis of health, and the absence of them will wreak havoc on your body.

Probiotics--I'll bet you didn't know that bacteria outnumber your body's cells on a ratio of ten to one. It's true. Your gut-healthy intestinal bacteria and a few friendly yeasts are all-stars, assisting players in synthesizing important chemicals for your brain, In addition to synthesizing serotonin, they perform a number of other healthy functions within your body, and scientists are still struggling to ascertain all the facts.

That hasn't stopped the public from jumping on the probiotic bandwagon. In 2012 the National Institute of Health reported that four million United States adults reported taking probiotic supplements. Even more revealing, 300,000 children had been given probiotics by their parents or caregivers. These health-conscious people read the emerging research and were quick to jump on the bandwagon.

According to Wang and Shurtleff, "The community of microorganisms that lives on us and in us is called the "microbiome," and it's a hot topic for research. The Human Microbiome Project, supported by the National Institutes of Health (NIH) from 2007 to 2016, played a key role in this research by mapping the normal bacteria that live in and on the healthy human body. With this understanding of a normal microbiome as the basis, researchers around the world, including many supported by NIH, are now exploring the links between changes in the microbiome and various diseases. They're also developing new therapeutic approaches designed to modify the microbiome to treat disease and support health."

Here is what the NIH has to say: They *may* support the cultivation of healthy bacteria in the body. They *may* influence your body's immune response. They *may* help relieve chronic pelvic pain. In other words, too little is known to make any veritable claims. But it's not too soon to eat more foods rich in probiotics, foods like Greek yogurt, dark chocolate, and pickles. Several, not so surprising, foods from abroad are included: miso, kefir, and kimchi.

Salt--Even the ancients recognized the value of salt. Early Roman soldiers were paid in salt, and hence the term 'worth one's salt' came into being. Salt was known as a preservative, and foods were salted to preserve them for another season.

Your body needs salt, but in reality, you're probably eating way too much. Processed foods are saturated with salt, and the average person consumes 77% of their daily salt intake in things like bread and chips. In addition, we've grown accustomed to salting our food as a matter of course. What happens when you ingest too much salt?

- Hypernatremia--in medicalese, this is too much sodium in the bloodstream, and it's seen when a person is severely dehydrated or has consumed too much salt. Symptoms include feeling irritable, having muscle cramps, acting confused, experiencing depression, and vomiting. Intravenous fluids are needed to rehydrate the body as quickly as possible.

- Bloating, which we all experience when we over-indulge in salty foods.

- Thirst

Here's what happens when you get too much salt in your system. Upon digestion, it moves into your bloodstream, and cells try to offload the excess into cells throughout the body. To keep your system in balance, you have to retain water, hence the bloating. All that extra fluid is hard on the lining of your blood vessels, and they become more rigid as time progresses, leading to high blood pressure. You've been eating your way blithely along and one day it will catch up with you in some rather serious consequences.

All of this shuffling of the unwanted sodium (from the salt, a compound of sodium chloride) is designed to keep you alive, my friend.

Your body maintains a very delicate dance called homeostasis. You must have sodium and potassium for normal transport of materials in and out of each cell, and your bloodstream carries fluid to help in the process. To maintain this delicate balance your body has a pump managed by an enzyme labeled adenosine triphosphatase. It pumps sodium out of the cells while pumping potassium into the cells. All of this takes place to ensure levels required to use glucose for energy.

To regulate the proper amounts of sodium and potassium, you will hear professionals talk about the DASH diet. It stands for Dietary Approaches to Stop Hypertension. It's simple, really. Eat less salt. Eat more foods rich in potassium. Those are vegetables, fruits, seafood, and dairy. Eat baked potatoes (as opposed to peeled potatoes), plain yogurt, salmon, and bananas. The biggest thing you can do is eat fewer processed foods, fewer salty foods, and banish table salt from the table.

Serotonin--This is chemically known as 5-hydroxytryptamine. It is a monoamine neurotransmitter, fancy jargon to say it works at nerve endings to create the safe passage of information from one nerve to the next. Think of a nerve as being a long tentacle of information stretching away from the brain. Each nerve has a head, a long body called the axon, and a tail. It has to connect to the next nerve in line to transmit information from the brain down to the heart, the lungs, the legs, to every part of the body. There is a smidge of dead space between these nerves, and the neurotransmitter carries the information across that space to the next nerve.

Beyond nerve transmission, serotonin affects many parts of the body. It helps control bowel movements, nausea, and diarrhea, with a direct link to irritable bowel syndrome (IBS). It regulates anxiety and mood. With too little, you suddenly get depressed. It's no secret it is the chemical responsible for good sleep. When you are wounded, your blood platelets release serotonin to help form clots and prevent hemorrhage. It plays a role in bone health, too. High levels lead to osteoporosis, which is a catch-22 for the elderly who experience trouble sleeping. Take just the right amount. It also affects libido.

We most often stress its role in good mental health. Reduce the need for big pharma in your life by regulating your mood naturally. Normal serotonin levels mean you feel happier, calmer and more focused.

Normal levels of serotonin are measured in blood tests and should be a level of 101-283 nanograms per milliliter (ng/mL). You don't need to know or remember this, but the salient point is that it is a chemical any lab can measure. If you think you have a high or low level, ask your doctor to order a test. A low level means you need to increase it, and medicine normally goes straight to the medicine cabinet. First, try increasing your exposure to bright light. Try regular exercise. Eat your way to higher levels with eggs, cheese, turkey, nuts, salmon, tofu, and pineapple. Try meditating each day.

Conversely, the opposite effect is caused by taking medications that result in an elevated serotonin level, known as the Serotonin Syndrome. Symptoms include shivering, diarrhea, headache, confusion, and dilated pupils. Untreated, it can affect voluntary muscles, evidenced in a high

143

fever, elevated blood pressure, a rapid or irregular heartbeat, and seizures.

When you can, eat your way to better health rather than going straight to the pharmacy and popping pills.

Sugar, sugar substitutes--Did you realize that sugar is a huge part of your diet? The daily recommended amount varies depending on which report you read, but let's say we're talking about 37.5 gm for men and 25 gm for women. That's about twelve teaspoons of sugar a day. What are most people actually eating? A person eating 2000 calories a day is probably ingesting 50 grams of sugar. Wowsers! Some researchers hypothesize the average adult is getting that 50 grams in *added sugar, hidden sugar* in addition to sweet indulgences

It's easy to recognize sugar in a can of soda. That's 39 gm in a twelve ounce can of Coke. Have that Coke with a bag of Skittles (another 47 gm) and you can see it add up. The problem is that those sweets are just the tip of the iceberg. Realize that unless you are actively avoiding sugar, you're probably eating way too much, and from sources never imagined. Almost every processed food includes sugar:

- granola

- protein bars

- yogurt

- bread

- tomato sauce

- canned soups

- processed nut butters

Become a label reader. You know to watch out for corn syrup and probably the "ose" words like fructose and maltose. Watch for fifty-six other words masquerading as sugar, things like fructose, sucrose, beet sugar, molasses, honey, caramel, carob, any kind of sugar or syrup, dextrin, dextrose, maltodextrin, D-ribose, galactose, agave nectar, turbinado.

Does it mean never having sweet treats? No. Look for stevia substitutes, like Lily chocolate. Use xylitol and other alcohol sugars, which are lower in calories and with fewer inflammatory effects on the body. Erythritol is made by a process of fermenting corn starch and it offers all the sweetness of sugar with only 5% of the calories. Sorbitol and maltitol are others. I use stevia and erythritol in 1:1 substitutions for sugar in my cookies, cakes, and bread with excellent results. Happy cooking!

Supplements--Scientists question the use of swallowing pills and supplements as a way of supporting brain health. Some push supplements and some question whether they are metabolized or excreted whole. No one offers any proof of their value. The craze for vitamins rose in the 1960s when Flintstones were peddled to children. Then One A Days became popular. These advertising campaigns legitimized supplementation and the public ran wild. Taking multivitamins evolved into taking a host of specific vitamins. I admit I've been caught up in the craze from time to time, taking E, C, B_{12} and

Biotin. I couldn't help myself. It's like the world has looked through the lens of crisis medicine, and, as a result, we all skitter around like chickens with our heads cut off, pecking at food supplements in hopes of warding off maladies like heart disease and dementia.

Probiotics are one example. The FDA regulates dietary supplements, but some probiotics don't require FDA oversight. Manufacturers may claim whatever they want without a slap on the hand as long as no health claims are made. No one knows if they help or hurt, but that isn't making any difference to some of the holistic healers prescribing them or the companies making them. The better alternative is a diet rich in nutrients, one I've been describing over and over throughout this book.

Since I concentrated on eating properly, rather than popping pills, I've been healthier and calmer. I've slept better and more consistently. I've learned to heal my body with foods as nature intended. This is Coach John talking: *Eat your way to better health.*

YOUR FREE GIFT

Thank you again for purchasing this book. As an additional thank you, you will receive an e-book, as a gift, and completely free.

This includes a fun and interactive daily checklist and workbook to help boost your productivity through simple activities. Life can get so busy, and this bonus booklet gives you easy and efficient tips and prompts to help you get more done, every day.

You can get the bonus booklet as follows:

To access the secret download page, open a browser window on your computer or smartphone and enter: **bonus.john-r-torrance.com**

You will be automatically directed to the download page.

Please note that this bonus booklet may be only available for download for a limited time.

RESOURCES

Berk, L.; Bruhjell, K.; Peters, W.; Bastian, P.; Lohman, E.; Bains, G.; Arevalo, J.; Cole, S. (2018, April 20). *Dark Chocolate Effects on Human Gene Expression.* Federation of American Societies for Experimental Biology. Abstract No. 755.1. Retrieved December 22, 2019 from

https://www.fasebj.org/doi/10.1096/fasebj.2018.32.1_supplement.755.1

Borelli, L. (2017, July 7). *6 Benefits of Eating Blueberries for Brain Health, From Lowering Dementia Risk to Improving Memory.* Medical Daily. Retrieved December 22, 2019 from

https://www.medicaldaily.com/6-benefits-eating-blueberries-brain-health-lowering-dementia-risk-improving-419938

Bowden Ph.D., CNS, J. (2018, August 16). *Clean Eating Is Not Disordered.* Clean Eating. Retrieved December 22, 2019 from

https://www.cleaneatingmag.com/author/jonny-bowden-phd-cns

DiSalvo, D. (2017, April 27). *Why is Diet Soda So Bad For Your Brain?* Forbes. Retrieved December 22, 2019 from.

https://www.forbes.com/sites/daviddisalvo/2017/04/27/why-is-diet-soda-so-bad-for-your-brain/#42bd7c885fad

Reviewed by Freeborn Ph.D., D., Cunningham, L., LoCicero MD, R, Updated by Rogers, K. (2018, October 18). White Blood Cell. (

Encyclopedia Britannica. Retrieved December 22, 2019 from
https://www.britannica.com/science/white-blood-cell

Greenberg Ph.D., M. (2015, February 5). *Why Our Brains Love Sugar--and Our Bodies Don't.* Psychology Today. Retrieved December 22, 2019 from https://www.psychologytoday.com/us/blog/the-mindful-self-express/201302/why-our-brains-love-sugar-and-why-our-bodies-dont

Higdon, J. (2005). Flavonoids. Oregon State University. Updated February, 2016. Retrieved December 22, 2019 from https://lpi.oregonstate.edu/mic/dietary-factors/phytochemicals/flavonoids#subclasses

Jeaveans, Christine. (2014, June 26.) How Much Sugar Do We Eat? BBC News. Retrieved December 22, 2019 from https://www.bbc.com/news

Lally, P.; van Jaarsveld, C.; Potts, H..; Wardle, J. (2009, July 16). *How Are Habits Formed: Modelling Habit Formation in the Real World.* European Journal of Social Psychology. Retrieved December 22, 2019 from https://onlinelibrary.wiley.com/doi/abs/10.1002/ejsp.674

Lappé, Frances Moore. *Diet for a Small Planet.* Ballantyne Books. New York. 1971.

Lehmen, S.; Fogoros, R. (2019, August 24). *Serving Sizes for Eighteen Fruits and Vegetables.* Very Well Fit. Retrieved December 22, 2019 from https://www.verywellfit.com/serving-sizes-for-18-fruits-and-vegetables-2506865

Levy CHHC, J. (2018, July 30). *Vitamin E Benefits the Skin, Hair, Heart, Eyes and More.* Dr. Axe. Retrieved December 22, 2019 from https://draxe.com/nutrition/vitamin-e-benefits/

Loma Linda University Health. *Dark Chocolate Boosts Memory.* Alzheimer's & Dementia Weekly. February 27, 2019. http://www.alzheimersweekly.com/2018/05/dark-chocolate-boosts-memory.html

McKay Ph.D., S. (2019, August 6). *Is Alzheimer's Disease a Women's Health Problem?* Your Brain Health. Retrieved December 22, 2019 from. http://yourbrainhealth.com.au/

Mosconi Ph.D., L. (2018, February 3). *Mind Food: What a Neuroscientist Eats.* The Times. Retrieved December 20, 2019 from https://www.thetimes.co.uk/article/mind-food-what-a-neuroscientist-eats-wd9mfz9st

Perry, D. (2018, June 7). *2 Rules for How to Cook Salmon Even Haters Will Love.* Real Simple. Retrieved December 20, 2019 from https://www.realsimple.com/food-recipes/how-to-cook-salmon-for-haters

Puckette, M.. (2016, August). Food and Wine Pairing Basics. Wine Folly. Updated October 30, 2019. Retrieved from https://winefolly.com/tutorial/getting-started-with-food-and-wine-pairing/

Rederer, M. 15 "Healthy" Foods You Won't Believe Are Full of Added Sugar. Health Prep. Retrieved December 22, 2019 from https://healthprep.com/fitness-nutrition/15-healthy-foods-you-wont-believe-are-full-of-added-sugar/?utm_source=bing&utm_medium=search&utm_campaign=328752049&utm_content=1146791188590073&utm_term=processed%20sugar&msclkid=d173b9d2037a12294431e42de10ac3f4

Shahzad MSc, A. (2018, July 24). Advances Along the Gut-Liver-Brain Axis in Alzheimer's Disease: Why Diet May Be So Impactful. Alzheimer's Association. Retrieved December 20, 2019 from https://www.alz.org/aaic/releases_2018/AAIC18-Tues-gut-liver-brain-axis.asp

Shute, Evan and Shute, Wilfred. Shute Vitamin E Protocol. Retrieved December 20, 2019 from http://www.doctoryourself.com/shute_protocol.html

Smith, K. (2017, May 13). *How to Eat More Brain Healthy Foods.* AgeRight.org. Retrieved December 20, 2019, from .http://ageright.org/2017/05/13/eating-more-brain-healthy-foods/

Sons, T. (2017, February 10). Supercharge Brain Health With These Foods. Retrieved December 20, 2019, from https://www.lifehack.org/530346/supercharge-brain-health-with-these-foods

Weiss, MD MCR, J., Woodell MD, T. (2019). Sodium Homeostasis. Chronic Disease in the Elderly. Retrieved December 22, 2019 from https://www.sciencedirect.com/topics/medicine-and-dentistry/sodium-homeostasis

Williams, R. (2012, January). Flavonoids, Cognition and Dementia: Actions, Mechanisms, and Potential Therapeutic Utility for Alzheimer Disease. Retrieved from https://www.sciencedirect.com/science/article/abs/pii/S089158491100 5764

Wang, Ph.D., Y. and Shurtleff, Ph.D., D. *Probiotics: What You Need to Know*. National Center for Integrative and Complementary Health. 2012. Retrieved December 22, 2019 from https://www.sciencedirect.com/science/article/abs/pii/S089158491100 5764

World Health Organization. (2013, August 28). WHO | Dementia cases set to triple by 2050 but still largely ignored. Retrieved December 20, 2019, Retrieved December 22, 2019 from https://www.who.int/mediacentre/news/releases/2012/dementia_20120 411/en/

Made in the USA
Columbia, SC
14 April 2022

58995793R00088